DOLCI

ITALIAN COOKING SCHOOL

WHITE STAR PUBLISHERS

DOLCI

ITALIAN COOKING SCHOOL

〉〉〉〉〉〉〉

❯ CONTENTS

Plate Desserts

❯ CONTENTS

Traditional Holidays with a Modern Touch

CARNIVAL

VALENTINE'S DAY

EASTER

HALLOWEEN

CHRISTMAS

› INTRODUCTION

Here you will find a rich selection of classic and sophisticated cakes, cookies, and desserts to spoil your family and friends with. A unique, must-have recipe book for LEARNING HOW TO MAKE a wide variety of delicious, tasty, and tempting SWEET TREATS that will fill your home with irresistible aromas. This indispensable book can be considered a kind of COOKING SCHOOL, where you can try your hand at all kinds of recipes, both easy and challenging. It will introduce you to the magical world of baking and no-bake desserts, teaching you all the BASIC TECHNIQUES and revealing ALL THE SECRETS YOU NEED to turn a textbook recipe into an unforgettable success.

Your first lesson will be to learn how to make the basic recipes needed for most of the recipes in the book, i.e., Dacquoise, Sponge Cake, Brioche Dough, Pâte Brisée, Choux Pastry, Sweet Shortcrust Pastry, and Puff Pastry.

In the next section, you will learn the TECHNIQUES FOR MAKING some of the great classics, most of which you will be familiar with: Melon Charlotte, Raspberry Meringue Cake, Mascarpone and Espresso Tiramisu, Panettone Zuccotto, Strawberry Mille-feuille, Semi-hard Wine and Anise Donuts, Summer Apricot Sachertorte, Blackberry Cheesecake, and Strawberry Paris Brest. These lip-smacking desserts are explained in great detail, step by step.

You will find a very satisfying selection of recipes under Small Pastries and Individual Desserts, perfect for those PANS OF SWEET THINGS we have all, at one time or another, offered as a gift to our host to thank them for their hospitality or received ourselves from a friend or relative.

These are the kind of sweet treats that are impossible to say no to when chatting with friends over a cup of tea or coffee, or when celebrating a special event: Diplomat Cakes with Vanilla Chantilly Cream, Puff Pastry Cannoli Cones with Custard Cream, Chocolate Mousseline Cream Beignets, Fantasy Eclairs, Banana Fritters on a Stick, Coconut and Almond Cakes with Strawberry Compote, Sweet Shortcrust Pastry Sfogliatelle, Mini Pumpkin Pies, Fruit Jelly Tartlets, White Chocolate Mousse Slices, to name but a few.

PLATE DESSERTS are next. Soft, fluffy, and creamy desserts are THE SENSUAL AND VOLUPTUOUS SIDE OF COOKING, ideal at the end of a romantic dinner but also great for tempting friends and relatives on any occasion. Get your whisk ready to whip up those light and frothy egg yolks and whites, essential for making these creamy delicacies. A few examples? Coconut and Mango Chiffon Cake, Sweet Vanilla Bavarian Cream Crescent, Rose Pavlova with Red Plums, Meringue Mille-feuille with Tea Cream, Chocolate and Hazelnut Truffle Semifreddo,

Lemon Pie with Double Shortbread, and Double Lemon Charlotte.

There is a mind-blowing selection of ULTRA-CHIC CAKES, rich in details and craftsmanship, with CAKE DESIGN DECORATIONS for show-stopping cakes to present on special occasions, birthdays, or important celebrations. You will be captivated by the elegance of the Chanel Cake, the colors of the Rainbow Crepes Cake with Coconut Cream, the detail on the Decadent Chocolate Cage Cake, the sophistication of the Mont Blanc, the grandeur of the Rocher Cake, the diversity of the Children Cake, and the pure temptation of the Seduction Cake.

Then, we move on to the section dedicated to scrumptious goodies for breakfast and yummy snacks. You will be enveloped by the DELICIOUS SMELL of freshly baked treats, piping hot cakes, pies, and cookies.

Page after page, you will become part of A WORLD BROUGHT TO LIFE BY THE SMELLS,

EMOTIONS, AND MEMORIES OF HAPPY BREAKFASTS AND TEATIMES: THAT WORLD OF BAKED CAKES AND COOKIES THAT MAKES US FEEL LIKE CHILDREN AGAIN. YOU CAN WAKE UP EVERY MORNING TO A HONEY AND WALNUT POUND CAKE, WHOLEWHEAT SHORTBREAD COOKIES WITH ORANGE MARMALADE AND APPLES, CARROT CLOUD CAKE, CHESTNUT FLOUR CAKE WITH CARAMELIZED PEARS, APPLE AND BLUEBERRY CAKE, BALOCCHI COOKIES, OR AN APRICOT AND RICOTTA BRAID. OR YOU CAN ENJOY A CUP OF TEA WITH RASPBERRY AND MILK CREAM ROLLS, WHITE CHOCOLATE, LIME, AND POPPY SEED SQUARES, APPLE ROSE TART, CITRUS-SCENTED SHORTBREAD COOKIES, OR WAFFLES WITH WHITE CHOCOLATE CREAM AND RASPBERRIES.

AND LAST, BUT NOT LEAST, SOME OF THE MOST TYPICAL HOLIDAY TREATS TO MAKE AT HOME LIKE A TRUE PROFESSIONAL. CHOCOLATE AND CINNAMON PASTRY FRITTER KNOTS WITH VANILLA CREAM AND PHYLLO PARCELS WITH CHOCOLATE ALMOND PASTE AND BANANAS FOR CARNIVAL; CHILI CAPRESE CAKE, CHOCOLATE HEART WITH TOFFEE SAUCE, AND RED VELVET CAKE FOR A ROMANTIC VALENTINE'S DAY; MINI GLAZED COLOMBAS AND NEAPOLITAN PASTIERA FOR EASTER; WITCH HAT COOKIES, SPIDER PUMPKIN CUPCAKES, AND BAT CUPCAKES FOR A CHILLING HALLOWEEN; AND A GINGERBREAD TREE, SPICED WHITE CHOCOLATE CAKE, PANFORTE, AND BINGO CARD COOKIES FOR A TRULY SPECIAL CHRISTMAS.

WHETHER YOU HAVE SOMETHING TO CELEBRATE OR JUST WANT TO TREAT YOURSELF AND THOSE YOU LOVE, ANY EXCUSE TO MAKE HOMEMADE CAKES, COOKIES, OR DESSERTS IS A GOOD ONE!

Basic Recipes

FLOUR, EGGS, MILK, SUGAR, SALT... THERE CAN NEVER BE TOO MUCH OF THEM. THESE ARE THE MAGIC FORMULAS FOR CRUNCHY, CRUMBLY, OR FROTHY BASES, AND SOFT OR CREAMY FILLINGS. AT TIMES THE RESULTS CAN BE HIGHLY ORIGINAL, BUT THERE IS ALWAYS A DELICIOUS, UNKNOWN ELEMENT THAT REVEALS ITS MAGIC WITH EVERY BITE. THESE BASIC RECIPES ARE PERFECT ON ANY OCCASION, WHETHER EVERYDAY OR SPECIAL: AT DINNER OR FOR A SNACK, FOR A PICNIC OR TEATIME, AT A BIRTHDAY PARTY OR SPECIAL EVENT. THERE'S SPONGE CAKE, A CAKE THAT HAS BEEN POPULAR WITH BAKERS EVER SINCE IT WAS INVENTED BY AN ITALIAN CHEF; BRIOCHE DOUGH, IDEAL FOR MAKING CAKES, FOCACCIAS, AND CROISSANTS; PÂTE BRISÉE, WHICH IS USED FOR VARIOUS RECIPES, LIKE BOAT TARTS OR TARTLETS FOR A DELICIOUS APERITIF; CHOUX PASTRY, LIGHT AND DELICATE FOR BEIGNETS; SWEET SHORTCRUST PASTRY, FOR PERFECT PIES AND CRUNCHY COOKIES; AND PUFF PASTRY, FOR MILLE-FEUILLES AND MOUTH-WATERING PASTRIES.

› DACQUOISE

INGREDIENTS
**for 3.3 lbs (1.5 kg)
of Dacquoise**
• 1 3/4 cups (400 g)
egg whites
• 1 1/3 cups (250 g) sugar
• 3 2/3 cups (375 g)
almond flour
• 2/3 cup (100 g) rice
flour

Beat the egg whites until stiff, gradually adding
2/3 cup (125 g) of sugar. Pour the almond flour
into another bowl, then stir in the remaining
sugar and the rice flour.

Add the beaten egg whites and slowly fold
into the mixture from the bottom upward,
so as not to break them down.

Line a baking tray with parchment paper
and draw 2 circles, using an 8 in (20 cm)
diameter bowl. Put the mixture in a pastry bag
and carefully fill in the circles.

Bake at 350°F (180°C), with the oven slightly open,
for 12 to 15 minutes.

serves 4

› SPONGE CAKE

In a saucepan, heat 1 cup (250 g) of beaten eggs
with just under 1 cup (175 g) of sugar and 1 Bourbon
vanilla pod, until it reaches a temperature
of 115°F (45°C).

Pour into a stand mixer and whisk, adding the sugar
a little at a time, until the mixture is light and frothy.

Remove the bowl from the mixer, add the sifted
flour and the potato flour, then fold them in
from the bottom upward.

Butter and flour the pans, then pour in
the batter. Bake at 375°F (190°C)
for 20 minutes.

INGREDIENTS
**for two 7 in (18 cm)
cake pans**
- 1 2/3 cups (150 g)
cake flour
- 4 3/4 tbsp (50 g)
potato flour
- 1 cup (250 g) beaten
eggs
- just under 1 cup (175 g)
sugar
- 1 pod Bourbon vanilla
- salt

TIPS
You can add various ingredients to the sponge
cake to give it different textures and flavors.
- Butter: Add it melted, but not boiling, at the end
of the preparation process, first to a small part of
the mixture and then to the rest. It should weigh 1/4
of the weight of the sugar. Butter improves the taste
and produces a crumblier, softer sponge.
- Cocoa powder: Its weight must be subtracted from that
of the flour, and the maximum quantity is 1 cup (80 g) to 10
cups (1 kg) of flour.
- Dark chocolate: This ingredient is also added melted and
in small quantities while making the sponge. As it is melted,
it must be mixed in before the flour and starch. The maximum quantity
is 7 oz (200 g) to 10 cups (1 kg) of flour.

serves 8

› BRIOCHE DOUGH

INGREDIENTS

for about 1 lb (500 g) of brioche dough

- 5 1/2 cups (500 g) cake flour
- 1/3 cup (80 ml) whole milk
- 1 1/2 tbsp (15 g) brewer's yeast
- 2/3 cup (180 g) beaten eggs
- 6.5 oz (180 g) butter
- 6 tbsp (70 g) sugar
- 2 tsp (15 g) honey
- 2 tsp (10 ml) rum
- 2/3 tsp (2 g) lemon zest
- 1/2 pod Bourbon vanilla
- 1/2 tbsp (8 g) salt

Pour the flour into a stand mixer.

Add the crumbled brewer's yeast, room temperature milk, beaten eggs, sugar, honey, rum, lemon zest, and the seeds from the Bourbon vanilla pod, then mix thoroughly for about 8 minutes.

Add the room temperature butter a little at a time.

Finally, add the salt and mix for another 5 minutes, until the dough is smooth and elastic.

Wrap the dough in plastic wrap and leave to rise at room temperature, until it has doubled in volume.

Deflate the dough by slowly kneading it by hand.

Wrap the dough in plastic wrap again, and leave it to rest in the refrigerator for about 3 hours before using.

serves 6

18   **PREPARATION TIME:** 20 min   **RESTING TIME:** 5 hours

› PÂTE BRISÉE

INGREDIENTS
**for a 9 in (23 cm)
cake pan**
- 2 1/4 cups (200 g)
cake flour
- 3.5 oz (100 g) cold
butter
- 5 tbsp (75 ml) water
- salt

Put the flour in a mixer with the butter
and a pinch of salt. Mix the ingredients
until you get a grainy-looking mixture.

Add the water and mix again until the mixture
has a smooth and elastic consistency.

Wrap the ball of dough in a layer of plastic
wrap; leave it to rest in the refrigerator
for at least 30 minutes.

Put the pâte brisée on a well-floured pastry
board and roll it out thinly with a rolling
pin.

Butter and flour a baking pan. Roll the pastry up
on the rolling pin and then unroll it onto the pan.

serves 6

PREPARATION TIME: 10 min   **RESTING TIME:** 30 min

› CHOUX PASTRY (OR BEIGNETS)

Basic Recipes

INGREDIENTS

**for about 1 lb (500 g)
of beignet dough**

- 1 3/4 cups (175 g)
all-purpose flour
- 5.8 oz (165 g) butter
- 5 tsp (25 ml) whole
milk
- 1 2/3 tbsp (20 g)
sugar
- 1 1/4 cups (270 g)
beaten eggs
- 3/4 cup (185 ml)
water
- salt

In a thick-bottomed pan, boil the water, butter, milk, and a pinch of salt.

When the butter has melted and the water is boiling, add the flour and sugar, stirring quickly with a wooden spoon. Leave to cook for a few minutes, until the mixture doesn't stick on the bottom of the pan.

Transfer the mixture to a stand mixer and knead it for 1 minute with the dough hook.

Add the beaten eggs a little at a time, until they are completely absorbed. Mix until the dough is smooth and glossy.

To make the beignets: Put the dough into a pastry bag and pipe balls, well-spaced apart, onto a dripping pan lined with parchment paper. Bake in a preheated oven at 425°F (220°C) for 25 minutes, until they are golden brown.

makes 50 small beignets

PREPARATION TIME: 30 min   **COOKING TIME:** 25 min

SWEET SHORTCRUST PASTRY

INGREDIENTS

**for a 9 in (23 cm)
baking pan**
- 2 1/2 cups (250 g)
all-purpose flour
- 4.5 oz (125 g) butter
- 3/4 cup (100 g)
powdered sugar
- 3 tbsp (40 g) egg yolks
- 1 pod Bourbon vanilla
- lemon zest
- pinch of salt

Put the all-purpose flour on a pastry board
and make a well. Add the powdered sugar,
egg yolk, chopped room temperature butter, salt,
lemon zest, and vanilla.

Work the ingredients into the flour
with your hands, until you obtain a sand-like
mixture.

When the dough is compact, shape it into a loaf
and wrap it in plastic wrap or parchment
paper. Put in the refrigerator to rest for at least
30 minutes before using.

Roll out the dough, then with the help of a rolling
pin, roll it out onto a previously buttered and floured
baking pan.

serves 6-8

PREPARATION TIME: 10 min   **RESTING TIME:** 30 min

› PUFF PASTRY

INGREDIENTS

for a 9 in (23 cm)
baking pan
- 2 1/2 cups (250 g) all-purpose flour
- 8.8 oz (250 g) butter
- 6 3/4 tbsp (100 ml) water
- salt

Put 1 3/4 cups (175 g) of all-purpose flour on a pastry board and make a well. Pour the water into the center and add a pinch of salt. Work the ingredients into the flour until you obtain a smooth and elastic dough.

Shape it into a ball and cut a cross in the surface. Wrap the dough in plastic wrap and leave it to rest for 30 minutes.

Pour the remaining all-purpose flour onto the pastry board, add the diced butter and work it into the flour until you obtain a lump-free, compact dough. Shape it into a square, then wrap it in plastic wrap and leave to rest for 5 minutes.

Take the dough without butter and roll it out fairly thinly. Put the square piece of dough in the center of the rolled out pastry. Fold the ends of the pastry over the square, then use a rolling pin to flatten it.

Fold the ends over the square again, then put the dough in the refrigerator for 30 minutes.

serves 6-8

Classic Recipes

In the delicious world of desserts, there are those great classics — "UNIVERSAL" RECIPES, SO TO SPEAK — that we are now all familiar with; they are part of our culture. And pastry chefs are no longer the only ones to have mastered these recipes, some of which are easier than others. Today, these recipes are part of every home baker's repertoire (often with even better results!), and they become very important when baking for HOLIDAYS, celebrations, and parties. We're talking about tiramisus and charlottes, cheesecakes and meringue cakes, mille-feuilles and sachertortes. However, while the joy of eating desserts is a SENSORY EXPERIENCE, also triggering emotions and memories, baking is AN EXACT SCIENCE. Ingredients, quantities, temperatures, and procedures are calculated with precise "formulas," which you must know and respect if you want good results. And, if you aspire to perfection, then following the instructions down to the last letter is actually indispensable.

› SEMI-HARD WINE
AND ANISE DONUTS

Put all the types of flour and sugar into a bowl, putting a few tablespoonfuls of light brown sugar aside, then mix them together. Add the oil and wine, then stir with a fork. Add the anise seeds and knead the dough by hand until it is smooth and uniform. Cover the bowl and leave to rest for 1–2 hours.

Make balls the size of a small walnut, then roll them into ropes with a thickness of about 0.5 in (1 cm). Wrap each one around two fingers, making the shape of a donut, and then close them by overlapping the ends.

Roll the donuts in the sugar you put aside, then put them on a baking pan lined with parchment paper. Bake at 275°F/140°C (on the middle shelf of a preheated oven) and cook for about 30 minutes, until the donuts have risen and are golden. Remove from the oven, transfer them to a wire rack, and leave them to cool. The donuts can be kept for a few days in a screw-cap jar.

INGREDIENTS
for the dough
- 2 1/2 cups (300 g) all-purpose flour
- 1/2 cup (70 g) whole grain spelt flour
- 1/2 cup (80 g) light brown sugar
- 6 tbsp (70 g) brown cane sugar
- 1/2 cup (130 g) white wine
- 2/3 cup (130 g) extra virgin olive oil
- 1 heaping tsp anise seeds

makes 35-40 baby donuts

> MELON CHARLOTTE

Pour the milk into a saucepan, add the vanilla pod
— cut lengthwise and with the seeds removed and set
aside — then heat. In a bowl, whisk the egg yolks,
sugar, and vanilla seeds until the mixture is light
and frothy. Slowly stir in the hot milk, then put back
on the heat and leave it to cook, allowing
the mixture to thicken but not boil.

Prepare the melon puree by removing the peel
and seeds from the melon half, then smash
the pulp with a fork.

Remove the saucepan from the heat and add
the gelatin sheets, previously soaked in cold
water, drained and thoroughly squeezed.
Stir in the melon puree and leave to cool.
Finally, add 3/4 cup (200 g) of whipped cream,
folding it in slowly from the bottom upward,
so as not to break it down.

Put an 8 in (20 cm) bottomless springform cake
pan on a serving plate. Cut the ladyfingers
to about 4 in (10 cm) long. Arrange them
on the bottom of the plate and along the inside edge
of the cake pan. Pour the mixture in and put
in the refrigerator to set for 6 hours.

Turn out the charlotte and decorate the top with dollops
of the leftover whipped cream and melon slices in the shape
of a rose, cut thinly with a mandoline. It is now ready to serve.

INGREDIENTS
- 3/4 cup (200 ml) milk
- 2 egg yolks
- 2/3 cup (130 g) sugar
- 1/2 medium melon
- 1 1/3 cups (300 g)
whipped cream
- 1/3 oz (10 g) sheet
gelatin
- 1 vanilla pod

you will also need
- 16 Sardinian ladyfingers
- 1/2 melon
- 1/2 cup (100 g) whipped
cream

serves 6

PREPARATION TIME: 1 hour   **COOLING TIME:** 6 hours

❯ BLACKBERRY CHEESECAKE

Classic Recipes

Finely chop the graham crackers and stir in the melted butter. Put an 8 in (20 cm) steel cake ring on a serving plate lined with parchment paper. Put the crackers inside and spread them evenly over the bottom with a spoon. Put in the refrigerator for 30 minutes.

Soak the sheet gelatin in cold water for about 5 minutes. Meanwhile, mix the cream cheese with the powdered sugar and vanilla extract, until the mixture is creamy and lump-free. Bring the blackberry puree to a boil, remove it from the heat, and add the drained and well-squeezed gelatin sheets. Leave to cool.

Slowly pour in the blackberry puree, stirring continuously. Finally, add the whipped cream, slowly folding it in from the bottom upward. Pour the mixture into the cake ring and put in the refrigerator to set for at least 5 hours.

Take the cheesecake out of the refrigerator, remove the ring, and gently peel the parchment paper off the plate. Decorate the top with fresh blackberries and serve.

INGREDIENTS
for the base
- 2 cups (170 g) graham crackers
- 3.2 oz (90 g) butter

for the cream cheese mixture
- 14 oz (400 g) cream cheese
- 1 pouch (100 g) blackberry puree
- 1 cup (140 g) powdered sugar
- 3/4 cup (200 g) whipped cream
- 2 tsp vanilla extract
- 1/3 oz (10 g) sheet gelatin

for decorating
- fresh blackberries

serves 6

› STRAWBERRY MILLE-FEUILLE

Classic Recipes

INGREDIENTS

- 3 x 15 in (40 cm) long rectangular sheets of puff pastry
- a little powdered sugar

for the lemon cream

- 4 1/4 cups (1 l) milk
- 3/4 cup (200 g) egg yolks
- 1 1/2 cups (300 g) sugar
- 1/3 cup (50 g) cornstarch
- 4 3/4 tbsp (30 g) all-purpose flour
- 2 cups (500 g) whipped cream
- 2 lemons
- 3 containers of strawberries

for decorating

- 1 sprig of mint

Once the puff pastry (made following the recipe in the first section of this book) has rested, sprinkle it with sugar and put it in a preheated oven at 375°F (190°C) for 15–20 minutes. Take out of the oven, leave to cool, and then turn it over. Sprinkle it with a little powdered sugar and bake again at 450°F (230°C) for about 4 minutes, until the surface is nicely caramelized. Remove, leave to cool, then cut into 15 in (40 cm) long rectangles.

For the lemon cream: Add half of the sugar to the milk and bring to a boil. In a bowl, whisk the egg yolks with the remaining sugar and the zest of 2 lemons. Add the sifted all-purpose flour and cornstarch, and stir thoroughly. Pour in the boiling milk and boil for about 5 minutes over low heat.

Put the cream in the refrigerator to cool. When it is cool, slowly fold in the whipped cream. Dice the strawberries, leaving some of them whole, and fill a pastry bag with the cream.

Build the mille-feuille by alternating the puff pastry rectangles with the cream and strawberries. Spread a layer of cream on the serving dishes and put the mille-feuille vertically on top. Using a pastry bag with a round nozzle, garnish the top with horizontal lines of cream. Decorate with mint leaves and whole strawberries, then serve.

serves 8

PREPARATION TIME: 1 hour   **COOKING TIME:** 35 min

> STRAWBERRY PARIS BREST

INGREDIENTS

for the choux pastry
- 8.8 oz (250 g) butter
- 2 1/2 cups (250 g) all-purpose flour
- 1 cup (250 ml) water
- 2 1/4 cup (525 g) beaten eggs
- pinch of salt
- pinch of sugar

for the cream and mascarpone mixture
- 1 cup (250 g) fresh cream
- 8 oz (250 g) mascarpone
- 3 tbsp (25 g) powdered sugar
- 1 vanilla pod
- 7 oz (200 g) strawberries

for the filling
- 1 egg
- a few feuilletine flakes (pastry crunch)
- powdered sugar

for decorating
- 2 oz (50 g) strawberries

serves 6

Put the choux pastry (made following the recipe in the first section of this book) into a pastry bag with a flat-topped nozzle, and pipe rings with a diameter of about 6 in (16 cm). Brush them with beaten egg, sprinkle with feuilletine flakes, then bake at 425°F (220°C) for about 15 minutes, or at least until the "rings" are golden brown on top. Remove from the oven, leave to cool, and then cut them in half.

Prepare the cream and mascarpone cream mixture: In a bowl, mix the cream with the sugar and the pulp of the vanilla pod. Fold in the mascarpone, using a spatula, and then whip with an electric whisk. Put the mixture in a pastry bag with a star nozzle, and fill the rings with rosettes.

Set aside a few whole strawberries. Dice the rest and arrange them on top of the rosettes, then cover with the other half of the ring. Garnish the top with a generous layer of cream and sprinkle with powdered sugar. Complete with a few whole strawberries, then serve.

PREPARATION TIME: 40 min   **COOKING TIME:** 15 min

› SUMMER APRICOT
SACHERTORTE

INGREDIENTS

for the sweet shortcrust pastry
- 7 tbsp (50 g) unsweetened cocoa powder
- 3 oz (85 g) butter
- 3/4 cup (100 g) powdered sugar
- 1 1/2 cups (125 g) cake flour
- 1 tsp (3 g) cake yeast
- 3 1/3 tbsp (50 ml) milk

for the dark chocolate mousse
- 1 1/4 cups (300 g) semi-whipped cream
- 1 1/4 cups (300 g) fresh cream
- 10.5 oz (300 g) 70% dark chocolate
- powdered sugar (to taste)

for the apricot jelly
- 1 lb 4 oz (500 g) apricots
- 1/3 oz (8 g) sheet gelatin
- 6 2/3 tbsp (80 g) sugar

for decorating
- 5 sliced apricots

serves 8

Prepare the sweet shortcrust pastry, following the recipe in the first section of this book, adding the unsweetened cocoa powder, sifted yeast, and milk to the all-purpose flour. This type of sweet shortcrust pastry does not require the use of eggs because they are replaced by milk, and it is a very soft dough. Knead it quickly to make a firm and uniform dough. Wrap it in plastic wrap, and leave it to rest in the refrigerator overnight.

For the jelly: Peel, pit, and dice the apricots. Blend them and then sift the puree. Measure out the required quantity. Heat half the puree with the sugar, and then add the gelatin — previously soaked in very cold water, drained, and thoroughly squeezed — and the remaining puree. Pour the mixture into dome-shaped molds and leave in the freezer overnight.

For the mousse: Heat the fresh cream with the chopped chocolate, then emulsify with an immersion blender. When the mixture has reached a temperature of 100°F (40°C), add the semi-whipped cream, folding it in slowly from the bottom upward. If you want to sweeten the mousse, add the powdered sugar to the hot cream.

Roll out the sweet shortcrust pastry between 2 sheets of parchment paper, to a thickness of 0.2 in (4 mm). Using an 11 in (28 cm) steel cake ring, make a circle of dough. Put it on a baking pan lined with parchment paper, and bake at 325°F (170°C) for about 25 minutes. Remove from the oven, take it out of the ring, and leave it to cool completely.

Cover the steel cake ring with a sheet of acetate, and line the edge with plastic wrap. Place the ring on a baking pan, put the sweet shortcrust pastry back inside, and put half of the mousse on top. Level the mousse, and put in the freezer for one hour. Put the apricot jelly domes on top, cover with the advanced mousse, and leave in the freezer overnight.

Take the sachertorte out of the freezer, remove the plastic wrap and the sheet of acetate. Transfer the cake to a serving dish and leave until it reaches room temperature. Decorate the cake with the apricots slices and serve.

› MASCARPONE AND ESPRESSO TIRAMISU

INGREDIENTS

- 1 lb (500 g) mascarpone
- 1 3/4 cups (400 g) semi-whipped fresh cream
- 6 tbsp (100 g) egg yolks
- 1 cup (200 g) sugar
- 1 2/3 cups (4 dl) cold espresso coffee
- 2 2/3 tbsp (4 cl) water
- unsweetened cocoa powder
- dark chocolate

for the ladyfingers

- 1 2/3 cups (350 g) egg whites
- 1 1/2 cups (300 g) sugar
- 3/4 cup (230 g) egg yolks
- 3 cups (300 g) all-purpose flour
- 1 1/4 tsp (4 g) lemon zest

for decorating

- unsweetened cocoa powder
- dark chocolate shavings

For the ladyfingers: Pour the egg whites into a stand mixer and start whisking. Gradually add the sugar as you go, and continue whisking until the mixture is creamy.

Add the beaten egg yolks, then the lemon zest, and finally the sifted all-purpose flour. Put the mixture in a pastry bag with a flat-topped nozzle, then pipe the ladyfingers onto a baking pan lined with parchment paper. Bake in a preheated oven at 350°F (180°C) for 10 minutes. Remove from the oven and leave them to cool.

Put the egg yolks in a bowl and whisk them with an electric whisk. Heat the water and the sugar over low heat, stirring occasionally. Bring the syrup to 250°F (120°C), and then slowly pour in the whisked egg yolks. Mix the mascarpone and cream together until you have a smooth cream. Slowly stir in the egg yolk mixture.

In an 11 in (28 cm) rectangular dish, do a layer of ladyfingers dipped in coffee. Cover them with a layer of mascarpone cream, followed by another layer of ladyfingers dipped in coffee. Repeat the sequence until the ingredients run out, ending with a layer of mascarpone cream. Put it in the refrigerator and leave to rest for at least a couple of hours. Serve out the portions, sprinkle with an abundant layer of cocoa powder, and garnish with a few chocolate shavings.

serves 6

PREPARATION TIME: 1 hour   **RESTING TIME:** 2 hours   **COOKING TIME:** 10 min

> RASPBERRY MERINGUE CAKE

For the cakes: Whisk the butter and sugar with an electric whisk until light and frothy. Add the eggs one at a time and continue whisking. Add the all-purpose flour and grated lemon zest, then stir by hand with a spatula. Pour the batter into 3 cake tins: 12 in (30 cm), 8 in (20 cm), and 4 in (10 cm), all buttered and floured. Bake at 350°F (180°C) for about 20 minutes. Remove from the oven and leave to cool.

For the buttercream frosting: Whisk the butter, powdered sugar, and vanilla seeds with an electric whisk until the mixture is frothy and creamy (hence the name buttercream). Put it in the refrigerator until you need it.

For the meringue: Put the egg whites in a stand mixer and whisk. As soon as they become frothy, add the sugar and continue to whisk until the mixture is firm. Pour the meringue into 3 different-sized bowls: put 3/6 of the mixture into the largest and add the dark pink food coloring; put 2/6 in the medium one, adding a smaller quantity of dark pink food coloring than you did for the first; put 1/6 into the smallest and add the pale pink food coloring.

Spread a thin layer of each meringue onto 3 baking pans lined with parchment paper. Bake at 180°F (80°C) until it is dry (if it darkens too much, lower the temperature and continue cooking). Remove from the oven, leave to cool, and then cut the meringues into different-sized pieces.

Cut each cake into 3 and fill each layer with the buttercream and raspberries. Put the 3 cakes on top of each other, with the largest at the bottom and the smallest on top, then cover the whole cake with buttercream. Garnish with the pieces of meringue, putting the darker ones at the bottom and working your way up with the other shades of pink. It's now ready to serve.

INGREDIENTS

for the cakes
- 18 oz (500 g) butter
- 2 2/3 cups (500 g) sugar
- 5 cups (500 g) all-purpose flour
- 10 eggs
- 3 lemons

for the buttercream frosting
- 21 oz (600 g) butter
- 9 2/3 cups (1.2 kg) powdered sugar
- 1 vanilla bean

for the meringue
- just under 1 cup (200 g) egg whites
- 2 cups (400 g) sugar
- pale pink food coloring
- dark pink food coloring

you will also need
- 1 lb (500 g) raspberries

serves 25

› PANETTONE ZUCCOTTO WITH CHOCOLATE MOUSSE AND ZABAGLIONE

INGREDIENTS

- 1 panettone

for the mousse
- 2 cups (250 g) fresh cream
- 1 cup (250 g) whipped cream
- 12.3 oz (350 g) dark chocolate chips (55% cocoa)
- 0.2 oz (5 g) sheet gelatin

for the cream
- 3 1/3 tbsp (50 ml) milk
- 13 1/4 tbsp (100 g) fresh cream / • 1 2/3 tbsp (20 g) sugar / • Just under 1/2 cup (125 g) egg yolks / • 4 1/4 tbsp (40 g) cornstarch / • 2/3 cup (150 g) Marsala wine / • 8 oz (250 g) mascarpone

for the syrup
- 2 cups (500 ml) water
- 3/4 cup (200 ml) rum
- 1/2 cup (100 g) sugar

for the black frosting
- 1 cup (125 g) fresh cream / • 5 tbsp (75 ml) water
- 6 1/4 tbsp (75 g) sugar / • 1 tbsp (25 g) glucose syrup / • 1 2/3 cups (300 g) dark chocolate

for decorating
- powdered sugar / • fondant icing
- green, red, and yellow food coloring

serves 6-8

For the mousse: Put 8.8 oz (250 g) of chocolate chips in a bowl. Heat the fresh cream in a saucepan over low heat. Add the gelatin, previously soaked in cold water, drained and squeezed; pour it over the chocolate chips and stir until they have dissolved. Finally, add in the whipped cream, folding it in from the bottom upward. Add the remaining chocolate chips, put the mousse in the refrigerator, and leave to rest for at least 3 hours.

For the cream: Whisk the egg yolks with 6 tbsp (70 g) of sugar. Add the cornstarch and then the Marsala wine, then whisk again. Add the milk and the remaining sugar to the cream and bring to a boil. Slowly pour in the whisked egg yolks, then heat until thickened, stirring constantly. Remove from the heat and leave to cool, then slowly add the mascarpone.

For the syrup: Put the water and sugar in a saucepan and heat until the sugar has dissolved. Remove from the heat, fragrance with rum, and leave to cool.

Line a 10 in (25 cm) diameter zuccotto mold with plastic wrap. Cut the panettone into 0.5 in (1 cm) slices, remove the crust, and line the mold. Put one circle of panettone on the bottom, then continue along the edge with more slices, without leaving any empty spaces. Wet with the syrup and proceed with the filling, alternating layers of mousse, panettone, and cream, and always wetting the panettone with syrup. Finish with a layer of panettone, cover with plastic wrap, put in the refrigerator, and leave to cool for 6 hours.

For the frosting: Heat the cream with the glucose syrup, water, and sugar. Pour the mixture onto the chopped dark chocolate and stir until it is dissolved. Turn out the zuccotto, transfer it to a cooling rack, and cover it completely with frosting. Put it in the refrigerator and leave to set.

Sprinkle the work surface with a little powdered sugar, then spread the fondant icing into a thin sheet. Cut out the shapes of the petals and leaves, and arrange them on a sheet of baking paper. With the leftover icing, make a few little balls, which you will color yellow. Color the leaves green and etch the side veins, then color the petals red to make 4–5 poinsettias. Garnish the zuccotto with the leaves and poinsettias, each decorated in the center with 3 yellow fondant icing balls. It is now ready to serve.

Small Pastries

and Individual Desserts

ᐱ

No Sunday lunch, birthday party, or dinner with friends or colleagues would be the same without small pastries and individual desserts, each UNIQUE IN ITS OWN RIGHT. They are the stars of those pans of sweet things we have all, at one time or another, offered as a gift to our hosts to thank them for their hospitality or received ourselves from a friend or relative. An afternoon break chatting over a hot cup of tea or coffee, or celebrating a special event, wouldn't be complete without them. And, when they are homemade, small pastries and individual desserts add a touch of ELEGANCE to any occasion. These include plates of delicious Fantasy Eclairs, inspired by those of the great French pastry chef Christophe Adam, or Diplomat Cakes with Vanilla Chantilly Cream, Puff Pastry Cannoli Cones with Custard Cream, and Chocolate Mousseline Cream Beignets, not to mention Coconut and Almond Cakes with Strawberry Compote, Sweet Shortcrust Pastry Sfogliatelle, and Fruit Jelly Tartlets. Thanks to the following recipes, you can have THE PLEASURE OF TRYING YOUR HAND AT MAKING ONE — or more — of these "treasure chests" of yumminess.

› CHOCOLATE MOUSSELINE CREAM BEIGNETS

INGREDIENTS

for the chocolate choux pastry
- 11 oz (310 g) butter (plus extra for the baking pan)
- 2/3 cup (150 g) beaten eggs
- 0.8 cup (2 dl) water
- 3/4 cup (75 g) all-purpose flour
- 4 3/4 tbsp (65 g) egg whites
- 1 1/2 tbsp (10 g) unsweetened cocoa powder
- 2 tbsp (25 g) sugar
- salt

for the chocolate mousseline cream
- 14 oz (400 g) custard cream
- 8.8 oz (250 g) milk chocolate
- 4.4 oz (125 g) butter

for decorating
- 5.3 oz (150 g) dark chocolate

Following the recipe for choux pastry in the first section of this book, add the cocoa powder to the sifted all-purpose flour and cook on the cooktop.

Take off the heat, leave to cool, and then add the eggs one at a time, stirring them in thoroughly. Put the dough into a pastry bag, then pipe lots of balls the size of a walnut onto a baking pan, previously buttered and floured. Bake at 425°F (220°C) for about 15 minutes. Take out of the oven and leave to cool.

Melt the chocolate using a bain marie.

For the mousseline cream: Whisk the custard cream with soft butter, add the melted chocolate, and stir thoroughly. Put the mixture into a pastry bag with a small flat-topped nozzle. Fill the beignets, dip the top in the melted dark chocolate, and leave to set on a cooling rack. They are now ready to serve.

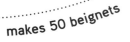

makes 50 beignets

PREPARATION TIME: 30 min   **COOKING TIME:** 15 min

› PUFF PASTRY CANNOLI CONES WITH CUSTARD CREAM

Small Pastries

INGREDIENTS

for the cannoli
- 10 oz (280 g) puff pastry
- 1 egg yolk
- 1 tbsp milk

for the custard cream
- 2 cups (1/2 l) milk
- 6 2/3 tbsp (80 g) sugar
- 2/3 cup (60 g) cake flour
- 4 egg yolks

for the dusting
- powdered sugar

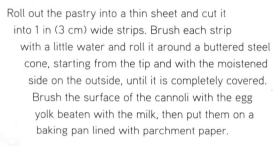

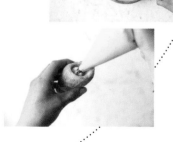

Roll out the pastry into a thin sheet and cut it into 1 in (3 cm) wide strips. Brush each strip with a little water and roll it around a buttered steel cone, starting from the tip and with the moistened side on the outside, until it is completely covered. Brush the surface of the cannoli with the egg yolk beaten with the milk, then put them on a baking pan lined with parchment paper.

Bake the cannoli at 400°F (200°C) for about 13 minutes. Take them out of the oven and leave to cool. Remove the cannoli from the steel cones.

For the custard cream: Whisk the egg yolks with the sugar until they are frothy; add the flour and fold it in thoroughly. Put into a saucepan, slowly pour the milk in, and cook, stirring constantly until the custard thickens.

Pour the custard cream into a bowl, cover with plastic wrap, and leave to cool. Put the custard cream into a pastry bag and fill the cannoli. Sprinkle with powdered sugar and serve.

makes 6-7 medium cannoli

PREPARATION TIME: 45 min   **COOKING TIME:** 15 min

› FIG CHEESECAKE
WITH GINGER AND ALMONDS

Small Pastries

INGREDIENTS

**for the sweet
shortcrust pastry**
- 4 cups (400 g)
all-purpose flour
- 6.3 oz (180 g) butter
- 2 1/2 tsp (20 g)
powdered sugar
- 2 egg yolks
- pinch of salt

for the filling
- 9 oz (250 g) cream
cheese
- 9 oz (250 g) quark
- 1/2 cup (50 g)
all-purpose flour
- 1/4 cup (50 g) sugar
- 4 eggs

for the fig compote
- 1 lb 4 oz (500 g)
peeled figs
- 1/2 cup (100 g) sugar
- 1 cup (100 g) flaked
almonds
- 1 ginger root
- butter

Prepare the sweet shortcrust pastry following
the recipe in the first section of this book. Shape it
into a ball, wrap in plastic wrap, and leave to rest
in the refrigerator for about 2 hours.

For the filling: Put the egg whites to one side
and whisk the yolks with half of the sugar,
then carefully add the flour and cheeses, stirring
thoroughly. Whisk the egg whites
with the remaining sugar until they are stiff,
then fold them slowly into the mixture.

For the fig compote: Toast the almonds in
a frying pan, and melt 1-2 tablespoons of butter
with half of the sugar in a saucepan. Add the
ginger, diced, and leave it to caramelize. Add
the figs and the remaining sugar, then cook for
about 15 minutes. When the compote begins to
thicken, add the toasted almonds, stir, and remove
from heat.

Roll out the sweet shortcrust pastry to a thickness
of 1/4 in (1/2 cm), then line the muffin molds
with the pastry. Divide the fig compote between
the tarts, then cover with a full tablespoon of filling. Bake
at 325°F (170°C) for about 30 minutes. Take out of the oven,
remove from the pan, and leave to cool. Top them with another
tablespoon of fig compote and serve.

makes 12 cheesecakes

> DIPLOMAT CAKES WITH VANILLA CHANTILLY CREAM

Small Pastries

INGREDIENTS

for the caramelized pastry
- 8.75 oz (250 g) puff pastry
- 9 1/4 tbsp (75 g) powdered sugar

for the rum syrup
- 1/4 cup (50 g) 70% liquid sugar
- 3 1/3 tbsp (50 ml) water
- 2 2/3 tsp (13 ml) rum

for the filling
- 17.5 oz (500 g) vanilla Chantilly cream
- 70.5 oz (200 g) sponge cake
- powdered sugar

Roll out the puff pastry to a thickness of 0.1 in (2 mm) and divide into two 9 x 7 in (23 x 18 cm) rectangles. Prick them with a fork, transfer them to a baking pan lined with parchment paper, and bake at 325°F (160°C) until golden brown. Remove from the oven, sprinkle with powdered sugar, then bake again at 100°F (40°C) until completely caramelized.

For the syrup: Put the water and sugar in a saucepan and heat until the sugar is fully dissolved. Take off the heat as soon as the mixture thickens and add the rum. Cut the sponge cake to obtain a rectangle that is slightly bigger than the puff pastry rectangles (about 0.2 in/5 mm bigger on all sides).

Put one of the puff pastry rectangles on a serving plate. Coat it with a thin layer of Chantilly cream, stopping at least 0.2 in (5 mm) from the edges. Put the sponge cake on top and moisten it with the syrup. Cover with a layer of Chantilly cream and then put the remaining puff pastry rectangle on top. Sprinkle with an abundant layer of powdered sugar, cut into squares, and serve.

makes 6 medium diplomat cakes

PREPARATION TIME: 40 min   **COOKING TIME:** 20 min

> FANTASY ECLAIRS

INGREDIENTS

for the eclairs
- 1/3 cup (80 ml) milk
- 1/3 cup (80 ml) water
- just under a cup (90 g) all-purpose flour
- 2 oz (55 g) butter
- 3 eggs
- 1 egg yolk
- 1 tsp sugar
- salt

for the filling
- 35 oz (1 kg) custard cream
- 2 sticks of instant coffee

- 1 lemon
- 3 1/2 tbsp (50 g) pistachio cream

for the coffee frosting
- 1 cup (125 g) powdered sugar
- 6 tsp coffee
- 1/2 tsp instant coffee

for the lemon frosting
- 2 1/3 cups (300 g) powdered sugar
- 1.7 oz (50 g) butter
- 3 tbsp lemon juice
- 1/2 tsp limoncello

for the pistachio frosting
- 10.5 oz (300 g) white chocolate
- 1/3 cup (80 ml) light cream
- 1/3 cup (80 g) pistachio cream

for the mixed berry frosting
- 7 oz (200 g) mixed berries
- 3 tbsp sugar
- 4 tbsp water

for decorating
- coffee beans
- lemon rinds
- ground pistachio nuts
- grated coconut
- red currants

Put the milk, water, diced butter, sugar, and a pinch of salt in a saucepan and bring to a boil. Take off the heat and sift the flour into the saucepan. Put back on a medium heat and cook, stirring continuously until the mixture starts coming away from the sides of the saucepan.

makes 16 eclairs

> > > > > >

Transfer the mixture to a bowl and leave it to cool. Add the eggs whole, putting them in one at a time and only adding the next egg when the previous one has been completely absorbed. When you have finished, the mixture must be uniform and smooth. Put it in a pastry bag with a flat-topped nozzle and pipe the eclairs, 0.5 in (1 cm) long, on a baking pan lined with parchment paper.

Brush each eclair with egg yolk and bake at 375°F (190°C) for about 20 minutes, until they have risen and are golden. Take them out of the oven and leave to cool.

Divide the custard cream between 4 bowls. Put one bowl aside. Add instant coffee, the zest and juice of one lemon, and the pistachio cream to the remaining three.

For the pistachio frosting: Melt the chocolate using a bain marie, add the light cream and the pistachio cream, then continue to cook over low heat until the mixture is the right consistency.

For the lemon frosting: Whisk the soft butter, sifted powdered sugar, lemon juice, and limoncello by hand.

For the coffee frosting: Add the liquid coffee to the instant coffee; add the powdered sugar and stir until the frosting is smooth.

For the mixed berry frosting: Put the water and sugar in a saucepan and heat until the sugar is fully dissolved; add the mixed berries and cook for about 10 minutes. Take off the heat and put to one side.

Using a knife, make small holes in the bottom of the eclairs.

Stuff every 4 eclairs with the different fillings.
Glaze those filled with plain custard cream with mixed berry frosting, and all the others with a different frosting. Garnish with coffee beans, lemon rinds, ground pistachio nuts, grated coconut, and redcurrants. Leave to set and then serve.

> PINEAPPLE AND WHITE CHOCOLATE MINI CAKES

INGREDIENTS
- 7 oz (200 g) pineapple pulp
- 2 eggs
- 1/2 cup (100 g) sugar
- 1/3 cup (80 g) seed oil
- 1 3/4 cups (170 g) all-purpose flour
- 2 tsp cake yeast
- 5.3 oz (150 g) white chocolate

for decorating
- 2.5 oz (60 g) small pineapple triangles

Butter and flour 6 mini cake molds (3.5 x 2.4 x 1.6 in/9 x 6 x 4 cm). Whisk the eggs with the sugar until light and frothy, then add the oil and the flour, sifted with the yeast, and mix thoroughly.

Dice the pineapple and blend it in a mixer. Add the pineapple puree to the batter and stir again. Divide the batter between the previously buttered and floured molds, filling them to 0.5 in (1 cm) from the top. Bake at 325°F (170°C) for about 35 minutes (use a toothpick to see if they are cooked). Remove from the oven and leave to cool.

Melt the chocolate and slowly pour it over the mini cakes, covering the top. Leave to set, then garnish each cake with a pineapple triangle and serve.

makes 6 mini cakes

› MINI PUMPKIN PIES

Individual Desserts

INGREDIENTS
• 3 1/3 tbsp (40 g) sugar
• 2 oz (60 g) butter
(plus extra for the molds)
• 1 large egg yolk
• 1 cup (100 g)
all-purpose flour
• zest of 1/2 grated orange
• pinch of salt
for the filling
• 4.5 oz (125 g) cooked
pumpkin (about
12–14 oz/350–400 g
raw pumpkin)
• 3 1/3 tbsp (40 g)
brown sugar
• 2 1/2 tsp (10 g)
castor sugar
• 1 medium egg
• 1/3 cup (40 g)
fresh cream
• ground cinnamon
for decorating
• 2/3 cup (150 ml)
fresh cream
• ground cinnamon
• 2 orange rinds
• powdered sugar

Prepare the sweet shortcrust pastry following the recipe
in the first section of this book, using orange zest instead
of lemon zest. Shape it into a ball, wrap it in plastic wrap,
and leave it to rest in the refrigerator for one hour.

Roll out the dough to a thickness of approximately 0.2 in
(4 mm), then line 4 well-buttered and floured pie molds
(leave a border of about 1 in/2 cm high).
Prick the base with a fork and put in the refrigerator.

For the filling: Put the cooked pumpkin in a mixer
and blend; add the fresh cream and blend for a few
more seconds. Lightly beat the egg with the two types
of sugar and a little cinnamon, then slowly pour it into
the pumpkin and cream mixture.

Bake the pies at 350°F (180°C)
for 7–8 minutes, then take out of the oven.
Put the pumpkin filling in and continue cooking at 325°F
(170°C) for about 20–25 minutes (use a toothpick to see
if they are cooked). Remove from the oven and leave to
cool. Whip the cream with a little powdered sugar.
Put the tarts on a serving dish and pipe whipped cream
rosettes on the top. Garnish with a sprinkling of cinnamon
and slices of orange rind. They are now ready to serve.

makes 4 pies

PREPARATION TIME: 45 min   **COOKING TIME:** 35 min

WHITE CHOCOLATE AND SOUR CHERRY MOUSSE WITH PISTACHIO BRITTLE

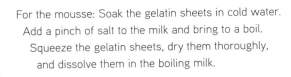

INGREDIENTS
- 13 1/3 tbsp (50 ml) milk
- 0.15 oz (5 g) sheet gelatin
- 7 oz (200 g) white chocolate
- 1 2/3 cups (200 g) fresh cream
- salt
- 5.3 oz (150 g) peeled pistachio nuts
- 1/2 cup (100 g) sugar
- sour cherries in syrup

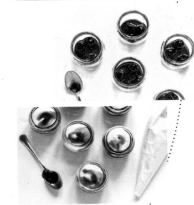

For the mousse: Soak the gelatin sheets in cold water. Add a pinch of salt to the milk and bring to a boil. Squeeze the gelatin sheets, dry them thoroughly, and dissolve them in the boiling milk.

Finely chop the chocolate and put it in a bowl. Pour in the hot milk and stir until smooth and velvety. Cool to room temperature, or until lukewarm.

Semi-whip the cream and slowly fold it into the mixture from the bottom upward. Strain the sour cherries and put the syrup to one side. Put 2–3 cherries and a teaspoon of syrup into each glass. Put the mousse into a pastry bag and fill half the glass. Drizzle with another teaspoon of cherry syrup and add more mousse. Put the desserts into the refrigerator and leave to set.

Toast the pistachio nuts, and in another saucepan, dissolve the sugar. As soon as the sugar is caramelized, add the hot pistachio nuts and stir thoroughly. Spread the brittle onto a baking pan lined with parchment paper and leave to cool. Put the brittle on a chopping board and cut into pieces. Decorate each glass with the pistachio brittle and serve.

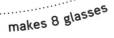
makes 8 glasses

❯ COFFEE SEMIFREDDO
IN A CUP

INGREDIENTS

for the semifreddo
- 6 2/3 tbsp (100 ml) milk
- 5 tbsp (75 g) espresso coffee
- 7 1/2 tbsp (90 g) sugar
- 3 egg yolks
- 1 cup (250 g) semi-whipped cream

for the cocoa wafer
- 10 1/2 tbsp (125 g) sugar
- 1/3 cup (35 g) all-purpose flour
- 2 tsp (5 g) unsweetened cocoa powder
- 3 1/4 tbsp (50 g) orange juice
- 1.2 oz (35 g) melted butter

for the coffee cream
- 13 1/4 tbsp (100 g) fresh cream
- 3 1/4 tbsp (50 g) coffee
- 1 1/2 tbsp (35 g) glucose syrup
- 1 cup (200 g) sugar
- just over 1/2 cup (65 g) unsweetened cocoa powder
- 6 3/4 tbsp (100 ml) water
- 2 tsp (10 g) coffee liqueur (to taste)

for the milk froth
- 1/2 cup (120 ml) milk
- 3 oz (90 g) lecithin

for decorating
- unsweetened cocoa powder

For the semifreddo: Add 5 tbsp (60 g) of sugar and the coffee to the milk and bring to a boil. Whisk the egg yolks with the remaining sugar, pour in a little hot milk, and then emulsify. Put the saucepan back on the heat and cook until it reaches a temperature of 180°F (82°C).

serves 6

69

Pour the mixture into a stand mixer and whisk until cool.

Slowly add the semi-whipped cream, folding it in from the bottom upward. Divide the mixture between the espresso cups (glass ones are best), leaving at least 1 in (2.5 cm) at the top.

For the wafer: Put all the ingredients in a bowl, stir thoroughly, and then put in the refrigerator to rest for at least 3 hours.

Roll out a thin sheet of dough on a baking pan lined with parchment paper, then bake at 350°F (180°C) for about 12 minutes. Take out of the oven and leave to cool.

Prepare the milk froth just before serving:
dissolve the lecithin in the lukewarm milk
and blend with an immersion blender until frothy.

For the coffee cream: Put all the ingredients
in a saucepan, bring to a boil, whisking
continuously with a hand whisk, and cook
for a further 2 minutes.

Put a tablespoon of coffee cream on top
of the semifreddo. Divide the milk froth between
the cups, decorate with a wafer and a sprinkling
of cocoa powder, then serve.

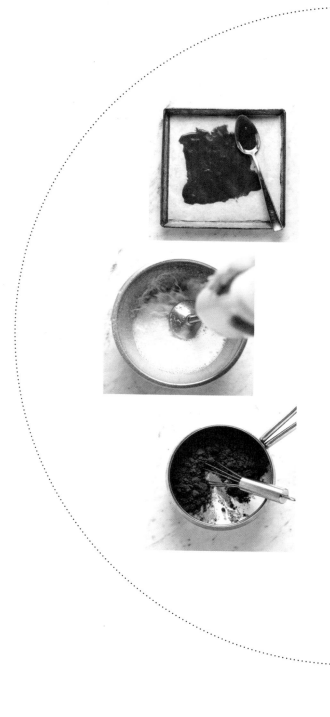

› SWEET SHORTCRUST PASTRY SFOGLIATELLE

Small Pastries

INGREDIENTS

for the sweet shortcrust pastry
- 2 cups (185 g) cake flour
- 4 oz (110 g) butter
- 9 1/4 tbsp (75 g) powdered sugar
- 1 3/4 tbsp (30 g) egg yolks
- zest of 1 grated lemon
- 1 Bourbon vanilla pod
- salt

for the filling
- 13 oz (370 g) sheep ricotta
- 2/3 cup (130 g) sugar
- 3/4 cup (187 ml) water
- 5 1/2 tbsp (60 g) semolina
- 2 tbsp (30 g) beaten eggs
- 1 cup (120 g) candied orange peel
- 1 tbsp (10 g) cornstarch
- pinch of salt
- pinch of ground cinnamon

for the garnish
- plum compote
- white chocolate
- pink iridescent food coloring powder
- edible gold dust
- edible gold leaves
- alcohol for cooking
- cold neutral glaze

Prepare the sweet shortcrust pastry following the recipe in the first section of this book. Make a loaf shape, wrap in plastic wrap, and then put it in the refrigerator for at least an hour.

For the filling: Pour the water into a saucepan and add the cinnamon and salt. Bring to a boil. Sift the semolina into the saucepan and cook on low heat for 5–6 minutes, stirring with a wooden spoon. Once cooked, spread the mixture onto a baking pan and leave to cool. Put it into a bowl with the sugar, cornstarch, and sieved ricotta cheese, and mix thoroughly. Finally, add the egg and chopped candied orange peel.

Roll the sweet shortcrust pastry out to a thickness of 0.1 in (2 mm), cut out lots of circles and line the half sphere molds. Using a smaller cookie cutter, cut out the same amount of circles as before. Put the filling in a pastry bag and fill the sfogliatelle. Cover with the smaller circles and press the edges firmly together. Bake at 350°F (180°C) for about 15 minutes. Take out of the oven and put in the freezer to cool.

Dilute the pink and gold food coloring separately in a little alcohol, then brush designs on a sheet of acetate. Glaze the sfogliatelle with chocolate: dip the bottom of the sfogliatelle (just less than half) in the melted chocolate, shake off the excess chocolate, and put them chocolate side down on the decorated sheet of acetate. Leave to set, remove the sfogliatelle from the sheet, garnish with the plum compote, and then glaze with the cold neutral glaze. Decorate with the edible gold and serve.

makes 12 sfogliatelle

> BANANA FRITTERS ON A STICK

INGREDIENTS

- 9 oz (250 g) strawberries
- 3 not very ripe bananas
- 2 lemons
- 1 sprig of mint
- coconut oil

for the mixed berry cream

- 10.5 oz (300 g) frozen mixed berries
- 2 tbsp brown sugar

for the batter

- 1 egg
- 9 2/3 tbsp (60 g) all-purpose flour
- 2 tbsp (20 g) cornstarch
- 1/3 cup (80 ml) cold milk (or lactose-free substitute)

for the sponge cake

- 4 eggs
- just over 3/4 cup (80 g) all-purpose flour
- 1/4 cup (40 g) potato flour
- 1/2 cup (100 g) sugar
- 3 tsp (20 g) raw acacia honey
- 1 tsp baking powder
- 1 Bourbon vanilla pod
- pinch of salt

serves 10

Prepare the sponge cake following the recipe in the first section of this book, adding the honey to the eggs, and the yeast to the all-purpose flour and the potato flour.

Pour the mixture into a 8 x 12 in (20 x 30 cm) rectangular cake pan lined with buttered parchment paper, and then bake at 325°F (170°C) for about 20–25 minutes. Remove from the oven and leave to cool. Turn out the sponge cake and cut it into squares.

For the mixed berry cream: Put the mixed berries and the sugar into a casserole dish and cook until all the fruit has softened. Put in a blender and blend until smooth.

For the batter: Beat the egg and milk in a bowl, add the all-purpose flour and cornstarch, and then mix thoroughly. Put in the refrigerator to cool.

Peel the bananas, cut them in half lengthwise and then into pieces; wet them with the juice of one lemon. Dip the banana pieces in the batter and fry in a non-stick pan with a little coconut oil, turning them carefully 2–3 times, until they are golden (it takes about 2–3 minutes). Drain and put them on a paper towel to dry.

Slice the strawberries, previously washed and with the tops cut off, and spray them with the juice of half a lemon. Slide the sponge cake squares, banana fritters, and strawberries alternately onto the sticks. Put the mixed berry cream into small bowls, garnish with mint leaves, and serve.

PREPARATION TIME: 40 min   **COOKING TIME: 30 min**

› FRUIT JELLY TARTLETS

Small Pastries

Knead the sweet shortcrust pastry a bit by hand, then roll it out to a thickness of 0.1 in (2 mm). Using a cookie cutter, cut out lots of circles. Line the tartlet molds, pierce the bottom with a fork, and then bake at 350°F (180°C) for about 15 minutes. Once cooked, take them out of the oven, leave to cool, then take them out of the molds.

INGREDIENTS
- 14 oz (400 g) sweet shortcrust pastry

for the chocolate and lime cream
- 2 cups (500 ml) milk
- 7 oz (200 g) white chocolate
- 1/2 cup (100 g) sugar
- 6 tbsp (100 g) egg yolk
- 5 tbsp (48 g) cornstarch
- 1 tbsp (10 g) grated lime zest

for the strawberry jelly
- 1 1/4 pouches (125 g) strawberry puree
- 2 1/2 tbsp (30 g) sugar
- 1 tsp (4 g) agar-agar
- 1 tbsp (10 g) dextrose
- pinch of citric acid powder

for the apricot jelly
- 1 1/4 pouches (125 g) apricot puree
- 2 1/2 tbsp (30 g) sugar
- 1 1/3 tsp (5 g) agar-agar
- 1 tbsp (10 g) dextrose
- pinch of citric acid powder

for the pear jelly
- 4.5 oz (125 g) pears in syrup
- 2 1/2 tbsp (30 g) sugar
- 1/2 tbsp (6 g) agar-agar
- 1 tbsp (10 g) dextrose
- pinch of citric acid powder

for the garnish
- 3.5 oz (100 g) cold neutral glaze
- 1.7 oz (50 g) white chocolate
- 6 1/2 tbsp (50 g) ground pistachio nuts

serves 10

❯ FRUIT JELLY TARTLETS

For the chocolate and lime cream: Pour the milk into a saucepan and heat. In a bowl, whisk the egg yolks with the sugar and cornstarch; add the mixture to the boiling milk and cook until it thickens. Take off the heat, add the chopped white chocolate, and then fragrance with the lime zest. Put the cream in a bowl, cover with plastic wrap, and put in the refrigerator to cool for 20 minutes.

PREPARATION TIME: 45 min   **COOKING TIME:** 15 min

For the strawberry jelly: Heat the strawberry puree. Stir in the sugar, previously mixed with the agar-agar and the dextrose, and leave to bubble for about 1 minute. Take off the heat and stir in the citric acid. Follow the same procedure for the apricot and pear jellies. Pour a layer of strawberry jelly into the cup molds and put in the freezer to set. Add the other two jellies in the same way, so as to create three layers, then put the cup back in the freezer.

Dip the edges of the tartlets first in the melted white chocolate and then in the ground pistachio nuts. Put the cream in a pastry bag and fill the tartlets. Decorate with a slice of the three-fruit jelly. Put in the freezer for 60 minutes and then glaze them.

› COCONUT AND ALMOND CAKES WITH STRAWBERRY COMPOTE

Small Pastries

INGREDIENTS

for the base
- 2 eggs
- 7 1/2 tbsp (80 g) peeled almonds
- 1 cup (80 g) coconut flakes
- 2.8 oz (80 g) butter
- 1/3 cup (80 g) full-fat white yogurt
- 6 tbsp (70 g) sugar
- 4 1/4 tbsp (40 g) cornstarch
- 3 1/3 tbsp (30 g) brown sugar
- 1 1/4 tbsp (12 g) cake yeast

for the strawberry compote
- 1 lb 4 oz (500 g) ripe strawberries
- 1 tbsp sugar
- juice from 1/2 lemon

for decorating
- 4 strawberries

For the compote: Chop the strawberries and cook them in a saucepan together with the sugar and lemon juice. Bring to a boil, lower the heat, and cook until the strawberries are soft, stirring continuously. Take off the heat, leave to cool, then blend them.

Put the almonds and half of the coconut into a mixer, and mix until you have a flour.

Put the butter, softened at room temperature, and the sugar in a bowl, then mix them until the mixture is pale and creamy. Add the eggs one at a time, then whisk in the cream. Add the yeast and cornstarch to the almond and coconut flour, then stir in the flour a little at a time, alternating with the yogurt.

Pour the batter into an 9 in (22 cm) square cake pan, previously buttered and floured, and bake at 350°F (180°C) for about 25 minutes, or until lightly golden (use a toothpick to see if it is cooked). Take out of the oven and leave to cool. Turn the sponge cake out and cut it into 20 equal-sized squares.

Spread a little strawberry compote on the top of each square, then put the squares together, two by two. Sprinkle with the remaining coconut, garnish with strawberries cut into 4 pieces, and serve.

serves 10

PREPARATION TIME: 30 min   **COOKING TIME:** 30 min

› WHITE CHOCOLATE MOUSSE SLICES

INGREDIENTS

for the biscuit
- 4 eggs
- 1 cup (100 g) all-purpose flour
- 6 2/3 tbsp (80 g) sugar
- 1 tsp cake yeast

for the white chocolate mousse
- 7 oz (200 g) white chocolate
- 1 lemon
- 6 2/3 tbsp (100 g) cream cheese
- 1 1/3 cup (300 g) whipped cream
- 6 2/3 tbsp (50 g) fresh light cream
- 2 containers of wild strawberries
- 0.2 oz (6 g) sheet gelatin

for decorating
- lemon rind
- powdered sugar
- wild strawberries

For the biscuit: Whisk the egg whites until firm. Add the egg yolks and all-purpose flour, mixed with the sugar and yeast, and mix thoroughly with a spatula. Pour the mixture into a baking pan lined with parchment paper and level. Bake at 350°F (180°C) for about 15 minutes (use a toothpick to see if it is cooked). Take out of the oven and leave to cool.

Cut two 4 x 10 in (10 x 25 cm) rectangles of biscuit. Line a 10 x 10 in (25 cm) rectangle steel cake pan with parchment paper, and put one biscuit rectangle onto it.

For the mousse: Soak the gelatin in cold water. Melt the chocolate using a bain marie, then add the lemon zest of one lemon and cream cheese. Bring the fresh cream to a boil. Drain and squeeze the gelatin, dissolve it in the boiling cream, then stir the mixture into the melted chocolate. Add the whipped cream, followed by the wild strawberries.

Pour the mousse onto the biscuit and cover with the second biscuit rectangle. Put in the refrigerator for at least 4 hours, and then in the freezer for about an hour. Take the cake off the baking pan and remove the parchment paper. Cut the edges of the cake with a sharp knife, then cut it into 8 slices and put them in the refrigerator. When serving them, decorate with a sprinkling of powdered sugar, slices of lemon rind, and a wild strawberry.

Plate Desserts

GET YOUR TEASPOONS READY, THE MOST DELICIOUS PLATE DESSERTS YOU CAN IMAGINE ARE WAITING FOR YOU: CREAMY UNCOOKED AND COOKED DESSERTS, COLORFUL BAVARIAN CREAMS, VIBRANT PAVLOVAS, FLUFFY CHARLOTTES, SEDUCTIVE TRUFFLES, REFRESHING SEMIFREDDOS, AND IRRESISTIBLE MILLE-FEUILLES. YOU WILL BE SEDUCED BY THE ENDLESS COMBINATIONS OF FLAVORS OF THESE SO-CALLED PLATE DESSERTS, BY THEIR SUMPTUOUS APPEARANCE, AND, ABOVE ALL, BY THEIR ENVELOPING CONSISTENCY. EACH DESSERT HIDES A SURPRISE THAT WILL TANTALIZE YOUR TASTE BUDS, WHICH IS WHY EATING THESE DESSERTS WITH A TEASPOON IS OF FUNDAMENTAL IMPORTANCE IF YOU WANT TO FULLY APPRECIATE THE FLAVORS. A WHISK, IS ESSENTIAL FOR MAKING THESE RECIPES, PRESERVING THE AIRINESS THAT GIVES THESE DESSERTS THEIR LIGHTNESS, VOLUME, AND BEAUTY. YOU CAN USE AN ELECTRIC HAND MIXER OR A STAND MIXER, OR JUST SOME GOOD, OLD-FASHIONED ELBOW GREASE: AS LONG AS YOU COOK ARTFULLY, EVERYTHING YOU MAKE WILL BE A SUCCESS. PLATE DESSERTS ARE EPHEMERAL — AS THEY ARE FINISHED IN JUST A FEW, DELICIOUS TEASPOONFULS — BUT DEFINITELY UNFORGETTABLE!

› SWEET VANILLA BAVARIAN CREAM CRESCENT

Plate Desserts

INGREDIENTS

for the crumble
- 7 tbsp (45 g) all-purpose flour
- 7 1/2 tbsp (45 g) almond flour
- 5 tbsp (60 g) brown sugar
- 2 oz (60 g) butter

for the vanilla Bavarian cream
- 5 tbsp (75 ml) milk
- 3/4 cup (100 g) fresh cream
- 2 tbsp (35 g) egg yolks
- 1 vanilla pod
- 0.1 oz (3 g) sheet gelatin
- 3 tbsp (35 g) sugar

for the raspberry cream
- 9 oz (250 g) raspberries
- 3 tsp (20 g) honey
- 1/4 tsp (1 g) xanthan gum powder

for the meringue
- 2 tbsp (30 g) egg whites
- 2 tbsp (25 g) castor sugar
- 1/4 cup (35 g) powdered sugar

for decorating
- 1 sprig of mint
- a few raspberries

serves 4

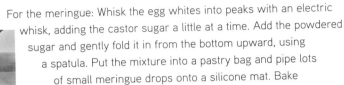

For the meringue: Whisk the egg whites into peaks with an electric whisk, adding the castor sugar a little at a time. Add the powdered sugar and gently fold it in from the bottom upward, using a spatula. Put the mixture into a pastry bag and pipe lots of small meringue drops onto a silicone mat. Bake at 212 °F (100 °C) for about 2 hours. Take them out of the oven and put to one side.

For the Bavarian creams: In a saucepan, heat the milk and vanilla seeds, without bringing to a boil. In a bowl, beat the egg yolks and sugar, then add the hot milk. Pour the mixture back into the saucepan and heat to a temperature of 180°F (82°C), stirring continuously. Take off the heat, stir in the gelatin sheets, previously soaked and squeezed thoroughly, and leave to cool. Whisk the cream with an electric whisk until fluffy, not whipped, and then stir into the custard. Divide the mixture between the silicone molds and leave to set in the refrigerator.

For the cream: Put the raspberries in a sieve and crush them with a spatula to obtain a puree. Add the honey and the xanthan gum powder, then blend with an immersion blender until the cream is thick and shiny.

For the crumble: In a bowl, mix the flour, sugar, and diced butter until the mixture is crumbly. Spread the crumble on a baking pan lined with parchment paper, and bake at 350°F (180°C) for about 10 minutes. Take out of the oven and leave to cool.

Divide the crumble between the serving dishes, in the shape of a crescent, then put 4 Bavarian creams on each plate. Garnish with dollops of raspberry cream, a few fresh raspberries, the meringue drops, and a few mint leaves. It is now ready to serve.

> DOUBLE LEMON CHARLOTTE

INGREDIENTS

for the biscuit
- 4 eggs
- 6 1/4 tbsp (75 g) sugar
- just under 1 cup (85 g) cake flour
- 4 1/4 tsp (15 g) potato flour
- 1 lemon

for the Italian meringue
- 1 1/3 cups (250 g) castor sugar
- 3 1/3 tbsp (50 ml) water
- 1/2 cup (125 g) egg whites
- salt

for the lemon mousse
- 3 1/4 tbsp (50 g) lemon juice
- 5.5 oz (150 g) Italian meringue
- 1 cup (250 g) semi-whipped cream
- 1/3 oz (8 g) sheet gelatin

for the lemon curd
- 4 tsp (20 g) filtered lemon juice
- 3 oz (85 g) butter
- 1/3 cup (68 g) sugar
- 2 egg yolks

for decorating
- 1 lemon
- small meringues
- ribbon

serves 2

For the biscuit: Whisk the egg whites with the sugar. Add the egg yolks, beaten with the zest of one lemon, and then mix in the all-purpose flour, sifted with the potato flour, with a hand whisk. Mix thoroughly and then put the mixture in a pastry bag. On a baking pan lined with parchment paper, pipe lots of diagonal lines, starting from the left corner. Bake at 350°F (180°C) for about 12 minutes. Take out of the oven, turn it upside down, and remove the parchment paper. Leave to cool, then cut it into 4 strips: 2x5 in (5x12 cm).

Line a 5 in (12 cm) square steel cake pan with plastic wrap. Line the edges with a strip of parchment paper, followed by the slices of biscuit.

For the meringue: In a saucepan, heat the water and sugar until they become a syrup. Whisk the egg whites with a pinch of salt until they are firm, then slowly pour in the syrup, at a temperature of 250°F (120°C), whisking continuously with the whisk on low-speed. Continue until the meringue is cold and shiny.

For the mousse: Heat the lemon juice, add the gelatin, previously soaked in cold water, and stir until it has dissolved. Fold in the meringue and the semi-whipped cream, then put it to set in the refrigerator for 4 hours.

For the lemon curd: Put half of the sugar in a saucepan, add the butter and lemon juice, then stir over low heat until the ingredients have dissolved. Mix the egg yolks and the remaining sugar, then slowly pour in the butter and sugar mixture, and mix thoroughly. Put the saucepan back on the heat and cook until the curd thickens. Take off the heat and leave to cool.

Put half a charlotte on each plate, fill each with mousse and then cover with lemon curd. Decorate with meringues around the dessert, and put 2 thin slices of lemon on top. Garnish with a ribbon and serve.

› COCONUT AND MANGO CHIFFON CAKE

INGREDIENTS
for the cake batter
• 6 large eggs,
room temperature
• 1 1/2 cups (300 g) sugar
• 3 1/3 cups (300 g) cake
flour
• 3/4 cup (80 g) coconut
flour
• 1 mango
• 1/2 cup (125 ml)
sunflower seed oil
• 1 packet of cake yeast
• 2 tsp (8 g) cream
of tartar
for decorating
• coconut flour

Put the two types of flour, sugar, and yeast
in a bowl, and mix with a whisk. As you whisk,
slowly pour in the sunflower seed oil and then
mix thoroughly.

serves 6-8

›››››››

91

Peel the mango, put a few slices aside
for the decoration, and blend the rest until
creamy. Stir it into the mixture. Add the egg
yolks, putting the egg whites aside, and whisk
with a two-whisk hand mixer.

Whisk the egg whites with an electric hand
mixer until they are very firm, then add
the cream of tartar: this is the secret ingredient
for a soft, well-risen dessert.

Add the egg whites to the mixture a little at a time, folding them in from the bottom upward so as not to break them down. The batter should be light and frothy.

Pour the batter into a 10 in (26 cm) chiffon cake pan, not buttered or floured. Bake at 300°F (150°C) for about one hour. Use a toothpick to see if it is cooked, and if it is not ready, cook it for a few more minutes.

Take the chiffon cake out of the oven, flip around the feet on the pan and turn it upside down, then leave to cool: when it has cooled down, it will separate from the pan on its own. Use a plate to help you turn it back over. Decorate with coconut flour and a few slices of mango, then serve.

PISTACHIO TIRAMISU SQUARE

Prepare the dacquoise following the recipe in the first section of this book, using pistachio flour instead of the flours recommended in the basic recipe. Pour the mixture into a baking pan lined with parchment paper, to a height of about 0.5 in (1 cm). Bake at 325°F (170°C) for 20 minutes. Take out of the oven and leave to cool. Then cut out three 8 in (20 cm) square dacquoise bases.

For the cream: Whisk together the mascarpone, fresh cream, and powdered sugar. Add the pistachio paste and mix thoroughly. Line an 8 in (20 cm) square steel cake pan with a sheet of parchment paper, put in one of the dacquoise bases, and cover with an abundant layer of cream. Put another base on top and cover with cream, then do the same with the third one, making sure you have a little cream left over. Put in the refrigerator and leave to set for at least an hour.

Take the dessert out of the cake pan and garnish it however you like with dollops of the remaining cream. Finally, decorate with white chocolate and a sprinkling of pistachio nuts, then serve.

INGREDIENTS

for the pistachio dacquoise
- 11 tbsp (150 g) egg whites
- 3/4 cup (150 g) sugar
- 1 1/2 cups (150 g) pistachio flour

for the pistachio cream
- 1 lb (500 g) mascarpone
- 3 1/3 cups (400 g) fresh cream
- 3 tbsp pistachio paste
- 3 tbsp powdered sugar

for decorating
- a few white chocolate
- pistachio flour

serves 4

PREPARATION TIME: 45 min   **COOLING TIME:** 1 hour   **COOKING TIME:** 20 min   95

› MERINGUE MILLE-FEUILLE WITH TEA CREAM

Plate Desserts

For the meringue: Whisk the egg whites with half of the sugar until very firm, then add the remaining sugar and slowly fold it in from the bottom upward. Put the mixture into a pastry bag and pipe lots of little squares, 0.2 in (0.5 cm) high, onto a baking pan lined with parchment paper. Bake at 225°F (100°C) for 2 hours. Turn off the oven and leave the meringues inside, with the oven door open, until they have cooled down.

For the tea cream: Bring the milk, fresh cream, and half of the sugar to a boil on medium heat. Take off the heat, add the tea and leave it to infuse for 5 minutes. Beat the egg yolks with the remaining sugar and the cornstarch. Filter the infusion, add it to the egg yolk mixture, and cook until the cream thickens; take it off the heat and leave to cool down completely. Add the gelatin, previously soaked in cold water then drained and squeezed, and the whipped cream, leaving a bit for decorating, and mix thoroughly.

Put a meringue square on all four dessert plates, cover each one with tea cream and a sprinkling of almond brittle. Cover with another meringue square and repeat as before. Add the last square and decorate with dollops of whipped cream and almond brittle, then serve.

INGREDIENTS

for the French meringue
- 3 3/4 cups (500 g) powdered sugar
- 1 cup (250 g) egg whites

for the tea cream
- 1 cup (250 g) whipped cream
- 3/4 cup (150 g) castor sugar
- 4 1/4 tbsp (40 g) cornstarch
- 0.5 oz (12 g) sheet gelatin
- 4 egg yolks
- 4 tea bags
- 1 1/2 cups (3.5 dl) fresh cream
- 1 1/2 cups (3.5 dl) milk

for decorating
- whipped cream
- chopped almond brittle

serves 6

> ROSE PAVLOVA
WITH RED PLUMS

INGREDIENTS
- 1/2 cup (110 g) egg whites
- 1 1/6 cups (220 g) fine castor sugar
- 4 3/4 tsp (15 g) cornstarch
- 1 tsp lemon juice

for the rose cream
- 1 cup (250 ml) milk
- 6 1/4 tbsp (75 g) sugar
- 2 egg yolks
- 3 1/4 tbsp (30 g) cornstarch
- 1 tbsp rose water
- 1 cup (125 g) fresh whipped cream

for decorating
- 3 roses
- red plums

Using an electric hand mixer, whisk the egg whites with the lemon juice until they are thick and frothy. Add the sugar, one tablespoon at a time, continuing to whisk until the mixture is firm and shiny. Sift the cornstarch into the egg whites, and fold in slowly by hand from the bottom upward so as not to break down the mixture.

Draw a circle with a diameter of 8 in (20 cm) on a sheet of parchment paper, then lay the sheet on a baking pan and pour the meringue inside the circle. Using a tablespoon, create a shallow well in the middle. Bake at 225°F (110°C) for about one hour and 15 minutes. Turn off the oven and leave the meringue to cool inside, with the oven door half open.

For the cream: Pour the milk into a saucepan and heat. In another saucepan, beat the egg yolks with the sugar, then add the cornstarch, followed by the rose water.

Slowly pour the hot milk into the egg yolk mixture, and stir continuously until the cream has completely thickened. Pour it into a container, cover with plastic wrap, and leave to cool. As soon as the cream has cooled, add the whipped cream, folding it in slowly from the bottom upward.

Wash the plums, remove the stones, and cut into slices. Spread the rose cream over the top of the pavlova, and then cover it with the plums. Garnish however you like with rose petals, and serve.

serves 4

PREPARATION TIME: 40 min   **COOKING TIME:** 75 min

› WHITE CHOCOLATE, LIME, YUZU, AND RASPBERRY SEMIFREDDO

Plate Desserts

INGREDIENTS

for the semifreddo
- 2.5 oz (75 g) white chocolate
- 5.5 oz (150 g) Italian meringue
- 1 cup (250 g) semi-whipped cream
- 2 limes
- 2 tbsp yuzu juice (Japanese citrus fruit)

for the Italian meringue
- 1/2 cup (125 g) egg whites
- 1 1/3 cups (250 g) sugar
- 3 1/3 tbsp (50 ml) water

for decorating
- 2 containers of raspberries
- a few lime rinds

For the meringue: Pour the water and 1 cup (200 g) of sugar into a saucepan and cook until it reaches 225°F (110°C). Put the egg whites in a planetary mixer, add the remaining sugar, and start whisking.

When the sugar syrup reaches a temperature of 250°F (130°C), slowly pour it into the egg whites and continue whisking until cool. Set aside 5.5 oz (150 g) of meringue for the semifreddo, and put the rest in a pastry bag with a 0.3 in (8 mm) star nozzle.

Pipe small meringues on a baking pan lined with parchment paper, and bake at 175°F (80°C) for about 30 minutes. Take out of the oven and leave to cool.

For the semifreddo: Melt the white chocolate, heat the yuzu juice and then add it to the chocolate, together with the meringue you put aside and lime zest. Mix thoroughly. Slowly fold in the semi-whipped cream from the bottom upward. Pour the mixture into a mold and put it in the freezer for 3–4 hours, until frozen.

Once frozen, put the semifreddo on a serving dish, decorate with slices of lime rind, fresh raspberries, and the small meringues, then serve.

serves 6

PREPARATION TIME: 40 min   **SETTING TIME:** 3-4 hours

› CHOCOLATE AND HAZELNUT TRUFFLE SEMIFREDDO

Plate Desserts

For the Italian meringue: Heat the water and sugar to 250°F (120°C). Start whisking the egg whites with the dextrose, then slowly pour in the sugar syrup and continue whisking until the mixture is lukewarm. Spread the meringue onto a baking pan lined with parchment paper, and leave it to cool down completely. Put it in the freezer.

For the chocolate semifreddo: Sift the cocoa powder into the custard cream, mixing thoroughly with a whisk. Slowly fold in the Italian meringue from the bottom upward, followed by the semi-whipped cream. Using a pastry bag, divide the mixture between the silicone molds.

For the hazelnut semifreddo: add the hazelnut paste to the custard cream, mixing thoroughly with a whisk. Slowly fold in the Italian meringue from the bottom upwards, followed by the semi-whipped cream.

Put the hazelnut semifreddo in a pastry bag, then pipe it on top of the chocolate semifreddo in the shape of a dome. Put the molds in the freezer. Once frozen, take the truffles out of the molds, roll them in the castor sugar and cocoa powder mixture, and serve.

INGREDIENTS

for the Italian meringue
- 12 tbsp (165 g) egg whites
- 5 tbsp (55 g) dextrose
- 1 1/2 cups (280 g) castor sugar
- 5 tbsp (75 ml) water

for the chocolate semifreddo
- 4 3/4 cups (570 g) 35% fat cream
- 10.5 oz (300 g) Italian meringue
- 3.5 oz (100 g) custard cream
- 1/4 cup (30 g) unsweetened cocoa powder

for the hazelnut semifreddo
- 2 cups (250 g) 35% fat cream
- 5.5 oz (150 g) Italian meringue
- 2 oz (50 g) custard cream
- 2 oz (50 g) hazelnut paste

for decorating
- 3/4 cup (150 g) castor sugar
- 1 1/3 cups (150 g) unsweetened cocoa powder

makes 10-12 truffles

PREPARATION TIME: 30 min   **FREEZING TIME:** 3 hours   103

› LEMON PIE
WITH DOUBLE SHORTBREAD

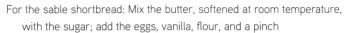

Plate Desserts

INGREDIENTS

for the sable shortbread

- 2.5 oz (75 g) butter
- 1/4 cup (35 g) powdered sugar
- 2 tsp (10 g) beaten egg
- 1 1/4 cups (110 g) cake flour
- 1 vanilla pod / • salt

for the whipped shortbread

- 13 oz (370 g) butter, room temperature
- 1/4 cup (60 g) egg whites
- 1 cup (150 g) powdered sugar
- 5 cups (450 g) cake flour
- 1 vanilla pod / • salt

for the lemon custard cream

- 6 3/4 tbsp (100 g) lemon juice
- 4 3/4 tsp (15 g) lemon zest
- 3/4 cup (170 g) beaten egg
- 3/4 cup (120 g) sugar
- 5.5 oz (160 g) butter
- 0.1 oz (4 g) sheet gelatin

for the whipped marshmallow

- 1.5 oz (40 g) marshmallows
- 1 egg white
- 2 3/4 tbsp (60 g) glucose syrup
- 5 tsp (25 ml) water
- 1/2 tbsp powdered sugar

for decorating

- puffed rice
- gianduja chocolate
- strawberries

serves 8

For the sable shortbread: Mix the butter, softened at room temperature, with the sugar; add the eggs, vanilla, flour, and a pinch of salt. Make the dough into a ball, wrap in plastic wrap, and leave in the refrigerator to rest overnight. Roll out the shortbread and cut out a circle with a 7 in (18 cm) cookie cutter. Put it inside a 7 in (18 cm) steel cake ring, and put a 4 in (10 cm) cookie cutter in the middle.

For the whipped shortbread: In a planetary mixer, whisk the butter with the sugar, the seeds of the vanilla pod, and a pinch of salt. Add the egg whites and continue to whisk. Add the flour and mix thoroughly. Put the mixture in a pastry bag with a star nozzle, then pipe a wave pattern around the edges of the shortbread and the cookie cutter, creating a space to fill with the cream. Put a strip of cardboard around both rings of piping, then bake at 325°F (170°C) for about 20 minutes. Take out of the oven and leave to cool.

For the custard cream: Beat the eggs and sugar together, add the lemon juice and zest, and cook until the mixture reaches the right consistency. Stir in the gelatin, previously soaked in cold water then drained and squeezed, followed by the butter. Fill the shortbread with custard cream and leave to cool, then remove the cake ring and the cookie cutter.

Prepare the whipped marshmallow: Whisk the egg whites with the sugar until firm. Put the water, glucose syrup, and marshmallows in a saucepan, and heat to a temperature of 260°F (127°C). Slowly pour the mixture into the egg whites, and beat with a whisk for about 5 minutes. Using a pastry bag with a petal nozzle, pipe the whipped marshmallow in a wave pattern on top of the custard cream.

Toast the puffed rice in a microwave. Melt and temper the chocolate. Add it to the puffed rice and mix thoroughly. Using two spoons, make lots of little puffed rice balls. Garnish with the puffed rice balls and strawberry halves, then serve.

PREPARATION TIME: 1 hour   **COOKING TIME: 20 min**

> BLACK COFFEE CAKE

INGREDIENTS

- 8 oz (250 g) mascarpone
- 7 oz (200 g) dark chocolate
- 1 heaping cup (110 g) all-purpose flour
- 9 tbsp (110 g) sugar
- 1 1/2 tbsp (10 g) bitter cocoa powder
- 4 tbsp ground coffee
- 3 eggs
- 6 3/4 tbsp (1 dl) cream
- 1 vanilla pod
- 2 tbsp (30 ml) espresso coffee
- 10 tsp (50 ml) rum
- salt

for decorating

- silver sugar cake decorations

Whisk the eggs with the sugar and a pinch of salt, until light and frothy. Continuing to whisk, add the cocoa powder, 2 tablespoons of ground coffee, the flour, and the seeds of the vanilla pod. Pour the mixture into a cake pan lined with parchment paper, and bake at 350°F (180°C) for about 30 minutes. Take it out of the oven, leave to cool, and turn out the sponge cake.

Put the mascarpone, 5 tsp (25 ml) of rum, 1 tbsp of ground coffee, and 2 tbsp (30 ml) of espresso coffee in a bowl, and mix until smooth. Cut the cake into two layers; put the first layer on a cooling rack, cover it with the mascarpone filling, then cover with the second layer. Put the cake in the refrigerator, covered with plastic wrap, for about 30 minutes.

Melt the dark chocolate with the cream and the remaining ground coffee and rum, using a bain marie, and mix thoroughly. Remove the plastic wrap from the cake and pour the lukewarm chocolate mixture over all the surface, using a spatula to distribute it evenly. When the chocolate has set, put the cake on a serving dish and decorate it with sugar decorations. Cut into slices and serve.

serves 8

PREPARATION TIME: 30 min   **RESTING TIME:** 30 min   **COOKING TIME:** 30 min

› PASSION FRUIT MACARON CAKE

For the cake: Cream the butter and sugar with an electric hand mixer until frothy. Add the eggs, putting one in at a time, and the chocolate, and continue mixing. Add the limoncello, flours, and lemon zest, and mix again. Pour the batter into a 9 in (22 cm) square cake tin, buttered and lined with a sheet of parchment paper, and bake at 325°F (170°C) for about 50 minutes (use a toothpick to see if it is cooked). Take out of the oven and leave to cool.

For the macarons: Blend the almond flour with the powdered sugar and sift twice to obtain a very fine powder. Mix 3 tbsp (40 g) of egg whites and a little food coloring, until you get the desired color. Add to the almond flour and mix thoroughly.

In a saucepan, boil the water with the sugar. When the syrup reaches 230°F (110°C), start whisking 3 tbsp (40 g) of egg whites. As soon as the syrup reaches 245°F (118°C), slowly pour in the egg whites and continue until the temperate drops to 122°F (50°C). Add the colored almond and powdered sugar mixture to the meringue, and mix thoroughly.

Put the mixture in a pastry bag with a 0.3 in (8 mm) flat-topped nozzle, and pipe 1 in (3 cm) diameter circles on a baking pan lined with parchment paper. Let the surface of the macarons dry for at least 20 minutes, then bake at 100°F (40°C) for about 13–15 minutes. Take out of the oven and leave to rest.

For the passion fruit curd: In a saucepan, melt the butter with half of the sugar and the passion fruit juice. Beat the egg yolks with the remaining sugar, slowly pour in the hot butter and sugar, and cook over low heat until the curd thickens. Add the gelatin, previously soaked in very cold water, drained and then squeezed, and leave to cool.

For the Chantilly cream: Whisk the mascarpone with the fresh cream, using an electric hand mixer, then put in the refrigerator. Cut the cake into 3 layers, then spread each layer with the passion fruit curd. Cover the outside of the cake with Chantilly cream, and decorate the edges with macaron halves. Fill the other macarons with passion fruit curd and put them on top of the cake. Garnish with flowers and serve.

INGREDIENTS

for the cake
- 8.8 oz (250 g) butter, room temperature
- 1 1/3 cups (250 g) sugar
- 6 eggs
- 3 cups (300 g) almond flour
- 5.5 oz (150 g) melted white chocolate
- 2 lemons
- 1/2 cup (120 g) limoncello
- 9 2/3 tbsp (60 g) all-purpose flour

for the macarons
- 1 cup (125 g) powdered sugar
- just under 1/3 cup (125 g) almond flour
- 2/3 cup (125 g) sugar
- 3 1/3 tbsp (50 ml) water
- 5 3/4 tbsp (80 g) egg whites
- orange food coloring

for the passion fruit curd
- 1/2 cup (120 g) passion fruit juice
- 18 oz (500 g) butter
- 2 cups (400 g) sugar
- 2 1/4 cups (240 g) all-purpose flour
- 2 gelatin sheets

for the mascarpone Chantilly cream
- 10.5 oz (300 g) mascarpone
- 2 1/2 cups (300 g) fresh cream

for decorating
- orange and yellow flowers

serves 4

> CHOCOLATE AND COFFEE TRUFFLE CREPE CAKE

INGREDIENTS

for the chocolate crepes
- 1 2/3 cups (150 g) cake flour
- 6 1/2 tbsp (45 g) unsweetened cocoa powder
- 2 eggs
- 1 1/4 cups (300 ml) milk
- 3 tbsp (25 g) powdered sugar
- 1-2 tbsp of butter

for the cream
- 14 oz (400 g) dark chocolate
- 10.5 oz (300 g) butter
- 2 tbsp (30 g) instant coffee

for the frosting
- 1/2 cup (60 g) fresh cream
- 2 1/2 tsp (12 ml) water
- 1 tbsp (12 g) sugar
- 1 2/3 tsp (12 g) glucose syrup
- 5.3 oz (150 g) dark chocolate

for the truffles
- 6 2/3 tbsp (50 g) fresh cream
- 5.3 oz (150 g) dark chocolate
- 1 1/3 tsp (10 g) glucose syrup
- 5 tsp (25 g) espresso coffee
- 1 tsp (5 g) coffee liqueur
- unsweetened cocoa powder

serves 6

Pour the flour and cocoa powder into a large bowl. In another bowl, mix the eggs with the sugar and milk. Add the mixture to the flour and mix thoroughly with a whisk. Cover and leave the batter to rest for at least 30 minutes. Melt the butter in a 9 in (32 cm) frying pan, then pour in just the right amount of batter to cover the bottom. Cook one side until golden brown, then turn it over and cook the other side. Remove from the frying pan, and continue to make more crepes until the batter is finished.

For the cream: Whisk the butter, softened at room temperature, with an electric whisk. Add the melted chocolate, at a temperature of 95°F (35°C), and continue whisking until the mixture is nicely frothy. Add the instant coffee and fold in with a spatula, from the bottom upward.

For the frosting: In a saucepan, bring the cream, glucose syrup, water, and sugar to a boil. Immediately pour the liquid into the melted chocolate, and stir the mixture with a spatula until it is smooth and shiny. Leave it to rest.

For the truffles: In a saucepan, heat the fresh cream with the glucose syrup and coffee. Add it to the melted chocolate, then stir with a spatula until the mixture is smooth and shiny. Flavor with the liqueur and put the mixture in the refrigerator to set. Make small balls, a little smaller than a walnut, and roll them in the cocoa powder.

Alternate the crepes with a thin layer of cream, until the ingredients are finished. Cover the top with a little frosting, letting it run a little down the sides. Garnish with the truffles and serve.

Having a Party?

The first decorated cakes were made in England in 1840, for the wedding of Queen Victoria and Albert of Saxony. The royal pastry chefs realized — almost by chance — that it was possible to create complicated yet delicate designs similar to ice (same shades and transparency) with a mixture of EGG WHITES AND SUGAR. Hence the name of one of the main ingredients used by cake designers throughout the world today: ROYAL ICING. In this section, dedicated to special and super special occasions, you will learn how to create three-dimensional objects and figures. You will master the art of SUGAR PASTE MODELING, of painting with food coloring, of making SUGAR FLOWERS (or entire gardens!), and of topping biscuits with the RUN-OUT technique. Needless to say, you will find some mind-blowing recipes here: flamboyant mini cakes and tiered cakes with phantasmagorical shapes and decorations, not to mention loads of IMAGINATIVE IDEAS for special occasions, holidays, and traditional and modern ceremonies.

> CAKE POPS DESIGN

Having a Party?

INGREDIENTS

- 14 oz (400 g) chocolate sponge cake
- 2/3 cup (150 ml) cream
- 10.6 oz (300 g) dark chocolate
- 2/3 cup (100 g) walnut kernels
- rum essence
- powdered sugar
- white, pink, and green fondant icing
- edible gelatin (or apricot jam)

Melt the chocolate using a bain marie. Put the crumbled sponge cake and the chopped walnuts in a planetary mixer; add the cream and blend until the mixture is smooth. Add the melted chocolate and the rum essence, then mix again. Put the dough in the refrigerator and leave to rest for about half an hour.

Once rested, take a little bit of the dough and make small triangles in the shape of a slice of cake, with a thickness of about 1 in (2.5 cm). Sprinkle the work surface with a little powdered sugar and roll out the white fondant icing. Spread a little edible gelatin or apricot jam on top of the slices, then cover with fondant icing. Repeat to create 3 layers for each slice of cake. Put strips of fondant icing around the layers to look like cream. Stick a toothpick into all of the cakes and put to one side.

Roll strips of pink fondant icing into small roses. Make little leaves out of the green fondant icing and draw the veins with a small knife. Put a little edible gelatin on the wide end of each cake, then put three small roses and a leaf on top. Leave to dry and serve.

You can use different colored fondant icing to "imitate" slices of cake filled with strawberry jam (red), or mint cream (green).

makes about 30 cake pops

PREPARATION TIME: 30 min   **RESTING TIME:** 30 min

❯ CHANEL CAKE

Having a Party?

In a planetary mixer,
whisk the butter
and sugar, then add
the eggs and flour, whisking continuously;
add the milk and then the yeast. Pour 3/4
of the batter into a buttered 10 in (26 cm) round
cake pan; add the cocoa powder to the remaining
batter and mix thoroughly. Pour it on top of the
batter in the cake pan, then bake at 325°F (170°C)
for 50–60 minutes.

For the buttercream: Whisk the butter, softened
at room temperature, with an electric hand mixer
until it is frothy. Gradually add the powdered sugar.

For the chocolate ganache: Bring the fresh cream to a boil
and pour it onto the dark chocolate, mixing thoroughly; stir
until the mixture is smooth. Stir in the buttercream.

INGREDIENTS

for the cake
- 6 eggs
- just under 4 1/2 cups (400 g) cake flour
- 2 cups (400 g) sugar
- 7 oz (200 g) butter
- 3/4 cup (200 ml) milk
- 2 tbsp unsweetened cocoa powder
- 1 spacket of cake yeast

for the buttercream frosting
- 7 oz (200 g) butter
- 3/4 cup (100 g) powdered sugar

for the chocolate ganache
- 6.3 oz (180 g) dark chocolate
- 1 cup (125 g) fresh cream
- 1 glass of buttercream

for decorating
- 7 oz (200 g) pink fondant icing
- 3.5 (100 g) brown fondant icing
- edible silver food coloring powder
- edible gelatin

you will also need
- powdered sugar
- mini silver sugar pearls
- a metal zipper

serves 10

Cut the cake into a parallelepiped, making sure that the sides are all parallel to each other. Cover the surfaces of the rectangle with the chocolate ganache. Sprinkle a work surface with a little powdered sugar, roll out 4 oz (100 g) of pink fondant icing, with a thickness of 0.1 in (3 mm), and cover the rectangle with it. Make sure it is well adhered to the ganache on all sides, and smooth the corners. Using a tool to create the quilted effect, draw lots of parallel lines on the longer sides of the cake, creating rhombuses. Cut out a triangle of brown fondant icing, stick it on the bottom right-hand corner of the rectangle with edible gelatin, and finish the quilted effect.

Using a sugar gun, make a long cord with the pink fondant icing, then stick it onto the front and back edges of the mini cake, to imitate the finishing edges of the bag. Roll out a thin sheet of brown fondant icing and cut out the "Chanel" logo, using two different-sized round cutters: cut out two circles with the largest cutter and then use the smaller one to cut out a circle in the middle. Remove a small section from the rings to make the 2 letters, overlap them, and stick them to the cake with edible gelatin.

Wash and dry the metal zipper thoroughly. Cover it with fondant icing and roll over it lightly with a rolling pin to bring out the details. Remove any excess icing, then color the zipper with the edible silver food coloring powder, previously mixed with a drop of water. To make the handle, use the brown fondant icing and etch the stitching effect.

Cut a piece of thick paper the same length as the handle, roll it up, and put it on the cake. Put the handle over it and use the gelatin to stick the ends firmly to each side of the mini cake. Wait at least 12 hours before taking the paper out. For the final touch, use the mini silver sugar pearls to finish the handle, by pressing them gently into each end.

> CHOCOLATE
CHARLOTTE

INGREDIENTS

for the chocolate biscuit

- 4 eggs
- 6 1/4 tbsp (75 g) sugar
- 14 1/4 tbsp (80 g) cake flour
- 4 1/4 tsp (15 g) potato flour
- 2 tbsp (15 g) unsweetened cocoa powder

for the chocolate cream

- 1 cup (250 ml) milk
- 4 egg yolks
- 1/4 cup (50 g) sugar
- 1/3 oz (8 g) sheet gelatin
- 3 3/4 cups (450 g) fresh cream
- 7 oz (200 g) dark chocolate

for the chocolate roses

- 15.5 oz (440 g) 55% dark chocolate
- 11 1/2 tbsp (250 g) glucose syrup
- powdered sugar

for decorating

- a cream ribbon

serves 6-8

For the biscuit: Whisk the egg whites with the sugar. When they are stiff, add the lightly beaten egg yolks and then stir in the flour, sifted with the potato flour and cocoa powder, using a hand whisk. Line a cake pan with a sheet of parchment paper, pour in the batter, and level until it is about 0.5 in (12 mm) thick. Bake at 350°F (180°C) for about 12 minutes, take out of the oven, then turn the biscuit upside down and remove the parchment paper. Leave to cool and cut two 9 in (22 cm) long strips.

For the cream: Heat the milk, then beat the egg yolks with the sugar until they are light and frothy. Slowly pour the hot milk in, then cook using a bain marie until the mixture reaches a temperature of 180°F (82°C). Take off the heat, add the chopped chocolate, and emulsify thoroughly. Stir in the gelatin, previously soaked, drained, and squeezed, and leave to cool until the mixture is 100°F (40°C). Whisk the fresh cream until it is 80% whipped, and then add it to the mixture, folding it in from the bottom upward.

Line a baking pan with a sheet of parchment paper. Put a 9 in (23 cm) steel cake ring on top; line the edge with a strip of parchment paper, followed by strips of biscuit. Cover the bottom with plastic wrap, pour in the chocolate cream, and put in the refrigerator for at least 6 hours.

For the chocolate roses: Melt the chocolate and the glucose syrup in two separate bowls, using a bain marie or the microwave, heating them to a temperature of 100°F (40°C). Mix them together and then leave to cool. Put the mixture in a food bag and leave it to rest overnight. Roll out the dough into a thin sheet, using a rolling pin and a little powdered sugar. Cut out circles with a cookie cutter and shape the petals; join them together to make the roses. Make the leaves, using a knife to draw the veining.

Carefully remove the dessert from the ring, then garnish the top with the chocolate roses and leaves. Wrap a ribbon around the biscuit and serve.

PREPARATION TIME: 45 min   **COOLING TIME:** 6 hours   **COOKING TIME:** 15 min

❯ CHILDREN CAKE

Having a Party?

INGREDIENTS

for the cake
- 12 eggs
- 8 1/3 cups (750 g) cake flour
- 4 cups (750 g) extra-fine castor sugar
- 26 oz (750 g) butter
- 3/4 cup (200 ml) milk
- 1 orange (juice and grated rind)
- 3 tsp cake yeast

for the buttercream frosting
- just under 7 cups (900 g) powdered sugar
- 16 oz (450 g) butter
- 1 orange

for the white royal icing
- 2 tbsp (30 g) egg whites
- 1 lemon
- 1 cup (150 g) powdered sugar

for decorating
- 7 oz (200 g) apricot gelatin
- 25 oz (700 g) white fondant icing
- 14 oz (400 g) white royal icing
- food coloring
- edible markers

you will also need
- 2 x 9 in (23 cm) cake pans
- 2 x 7 in (18 cm) cake pans
- 2 x 5 in (13 cm) cake pans

For the cake: Cream the butter, softened at room temperature, sugar, and lemon zest until soft and creamy. Add the eggs, flour, yeast, milk, and orange juice, and mix thoroughly. Divide the mixture between the buttered cake pans and bake at 350°F (180°C) for about 30–35 minutes.

For the buttercream: Cream the butter, softened at room temperature, and the powdered sugar until soft and creamy, then add the orange juice. Fill the cake, starting with the two 9 in (23 cm) layers, putting them directly onto the serving plate when they are ready. Level the edges and fill all the other layers of the cake.

Brush the surface of the cake with apricot gelatin and cover with white fondant icing. Make sure the icing is well adhered to the edges, then remove any excess icing. When you have covered all the layers, put them on top of each other using cake dowels.

For the white royal icing: Whisk the egg whites and a few drops of lemon juice with an electric hand mixer. Continue to whisk, gradually adding the powdered sugar, until the icing is smooth and shiny.

Use the colored fondant icing to make the children's clothes and faces, using different colors to represent the different nationalities. Do the children's hair with different colored royal icing. Use black royal icing or an edible marker to draw the details on the faces. Finally, make a doll with the fondant icing and put it on top of the cake.

serves 30

PREPARATION TIME: 2 hours   **RESTING TIME:** 1 hour   **COOKING TIME:** 35 min

» CORAL BAY

Whisk the sugar and eggs in a planetary mixer, then add the butter, softened at room temperature. Mix the flours, wheat starch, and yeast, and slowly fold into the mixture. Pour 2/3 of the batter into an 11 in (28 cm) round cake pan, previously buttered, and put the remaining batter into another one of the same size. Bake at 350°F (180°C) for about 35–40 minutes. Make the top layers of the cake in the same way, using 1/3 of the quantities given for the larger base, and round cake pans measuring 7 in (18 cm) and 4 in (10 cm).

Having a Party?

INGREDIENTS

for the larger base
- 10 eggs
- 2 1/2 cups (250 g) coconut flour
- 1 1/2 cups (150 g) all-purpose flour
- 2 1/2 cups (250 g) wheat starch
- 2 cups (400 g) sugar
- 8.8 oz (250 g) butter
- 1 2/3 tbsp (16 g) cake yeast

for the custard cream
- 1 cup (300 g) egg yolk
- 1/2 cup (50 g) all-purpose flour
- 3/4 cup (120 g) cornstarch
- 1 1/2 cups (300 g) sugar
- 3 1/3 cup (800 ml) milk
- 1 2/3 cups (200 g) fresh cream
- 1 vanilla pod

for the buttercream frosting
- 2 2/3 cups (350 g) powdered sugar
- 4.5 oz (130 g) butter
- 4.5 oz (130 g) margarine
- 3–4 tbsp milk

for decorating
- 1 whole pineapple
- 35 oz (1 kg) white fondant icing
- food coloring (brown, black, red, iridescent light blue)
- edible gelatin
- acetate cake wrap
- a piece of string

serves 20-22

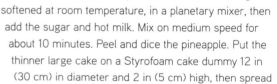
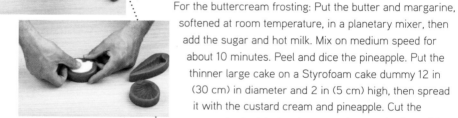

For the custard cream: Heat the milk and cream with the seeds of the vanilla pod. Whisk the egg yolks with the sugar, add the flour and cornstarch, then pour the cream into the boiling milk. Stir continuously for about 2–3 minutes and then take off the heat.

For the buttercream frosting: Put the butter and margarine, softened at room temperature, in a planetary mixer, then add the sugar and hot milk. Mix on medium speed for about 10 minutes. Peel and dice the pineapple. Put the thinner large cake on a Styrofoam cake dummy 12 in (30 cm) in diameter and 2 in (5 cm) high, then spread it with the custard cream and pineapple. Cut the second cake into two layers, and cover the first with custard cream and pineapple. Add all the other layers, spreading each with custard cream and pineapple, and then cover the whole cake with buttercream.

Roll out 28 oz (800 g) of fondant icing to a thickness of 0.1 in (3 mm), roll it onto the rolling pin and cover the cake, leveling the icing and removing any excess. With the remaining fondant icing make three balls: white, light brown, and gray (add food coloring to create the different colors).

Cut a little icing off each ball and mix them together, kneading slowly until you get the right level of marbling. Make a walnut-sized ball of white fondant icing and add a little bit of the marbled icing. Knead for a few seconds and then put in the silicone molds. Leave to rest for a few minutes, then carefully turn them out. Make more balls of colored fondant icing, and use molds to make corals, starfish, and the other decorations.

Attach the acetate cake wrap to the base of the cake, brushing it with edible gelatin, and cover it with a ribbon, followed by a piece of string. Attach the decorations to the cake with gelatin. Finally, make a small pearl with the white fondant icing, put it on top of the cake using gelatin, and color it with the iridescent food coloring.

PREPARATION TIME: 2 hours   **COOKING TIME: 40 min**

› MONT BLANC

Having a Party?

INGREDIENTS

for the sponge cake
- 1 cup (250 g) beaten egg
- 2/3 cup (125 g) sugar
- 1 1/4 cups (125 g) all-purpose flour

for the custard cream
- 2 cups (500 ml) milk
- 3/4 cup (150 g) sugar
- just under 1/2 cup (125 g) egg yolks
- 4 1/4 tbsp (40 g) cornstarch

for the Mont Blanc cream
- 2 cups (500 g) custard cream
- 5.3 oz (150 g) sweet chestnut paste
- 2 1/2 cups (300 g) fresh cream
- 1/4 cup (50 g) sugar

for the vanilla syrup
- just under 2 cups (350 g) sugar
- 1 1/2 cups (375 ml) water
- 6 3/4 tbsp (100 g) vanilla extract at 160°F (70°C)

for decorating
- tempered dark chocolate
- whipped cream
- unsweetened cocoa powder
- candied chestnuts

For the custard cream: Beat the egg yolks with the sugar and cornstarch. Heat the milk and slowly pour it in, mixing thoroughly. Cook the mixture until thick and creamy, stirring continuously.

serves 6-8

For the white Mont Blanc cream: Stir the sweet chestnut paste into the custard cream. Whisk the fresh cream with the sugar and fold it slowly into the mixture from the bottom upward.

Make the sponge cake following the recipe on page 16, only using the cake flour. Pour the batter into a 7 in (18 cm) round cake pan, buttered and floured, and bake at 350°F (180°C) for about 40 minutes. Take out of the oven and leave to cool.

For the syrup: Put the water and sugar in a saucepan. Bring to a boil, take off the heat, and leave to cool. Add the vanilla extract and stir again.

Cut the sponge cake into two layers. Wet the first layer with the syrup and cover it with a layer of Mont Blanc cream. Put the second layer on top, also wet with syrup, and cover with cream to create a dome shape. Put the whipped cream in a pastry bag with a serrated nozzle, and pipe vertical lines from the bottom to top. Finish with a dollop of cream in the middle of the top of the cake.

Melt the chocolate, put it in a pastry bag, and pipe lines on a marble surface. Leave them to set, then roll them into the shape of a nest and put it on top of the cake. Garnish with candied chestnuts and a sprinkling of cocoa powder, then serve.

❯ NUMBER CAKE

Prepare the sweet shortcrust pastry following the recipe in the first section of this book, but without the vanilla. Make a loaf shape, wrap in plastic wrap, and leave to rest in the refrigerator for at least an hour.

Prepare a paper template of the number approximately 14 in (35 cm) high. Roll out the sweet shortcrust pastry to a thickness of about 0.2 in (5 mm), and cut out two of the chosen number. Transfer them to a baking pan lined with parchment paper, and bake at 350°F (180°C) for about 10–12 minutes.

For the cream: Put all of the ingredients in a bowl and whisk with an electric hand mixer, until the mixture is thick and frothy, then put it in a pastry bag.

INGREDIENTS

for the sweet shortcrust pastry
- 8.8 oz (250 g) butter
- 15 tbsp (180 g) castor sugar
- 4 egg yolks
- just under 4 1/2 cups (400 g) cake flour
- pinch of salt

for the cream
- 4 cups (500 g) fresh cream (unsweetened)
- 14 oz (450 g) mascarpone
- 11 tbsp (90 g) powdered sugar

for decorating
- fresh fruit such as strawberries
- 3 flowers
- 3 macarons

Put one of the sweet shortcrust pastry numbers on a serving plate and cover with lots of dollops of cream, arranging them neatly and close to one another. Very carefully, put the second number on top (get someone to help you if necessary). Cover with more dollops of cream.

Decorate the cake with flowers, strawberry halves, and macarons. Leave the cake to rest in the refrigerator for 2 hours, then serve.

TIPS

- To make the numbers perfect, prepare the template on a Word file on your computer, using Word Art, and print it in a slightly larger format than a sheet of A4 paper (the numbers should be approximately 14 in/35 cm high and 9 in/23 cm wide). Choose a simple font with lots of space inside the number, and a calligraphy that isn't thin or complicated. • Make sure the numbers have cooled completely before removing them from the baking pan, otherwise they will break. They are very delicate, so ask someone to help you move them, and leave them on the parchment paper they were cooked on. • We recommend you assemble the cake directly on the plate you will be serving it on. • Before making the cake, always check that the plate fits in the refrigerator. • Macarons can be purchased ready-made from a bakery. • Once ready, this cake can be kept for a maximum of 2 days in the refrigerator.

serves 10

> RAINBOW CREPES CAKE WITH COCONUT CREAM

Having a Party?

INGREDIENTS

for the crepes
- 1 1/2 cups (350 ml) milk
- 1 2/3 cups (150 g) cake flour
- 2 eggs
- 2 1/2 tsp (10 g) sugar
- ground cinnamon
- food coloring (red, yellow, green, purple, blue, and orange)
- 1-2 tbsp of butter

for the coconut cream
- 1 2/3 cups (400 ml) coconut milk
- 3/4 cup (100 g) fresh cream
- 4 1/4 tbsp (40 g) cornstarch
- 6 tbsp (100 g) egg yolks
- 3/4 cup (120 g) sugar
- 3/4 cup (200 g) whipped cream

for decorating
- 1 1/3 cup (300 g) whipped cream
- grated coconut
- chocolate rainbow candy balls

Put the flour and 2 pinches of cinnamon in a large bowl. In another bowl, mix the eggs with the sugar and milk. Fold in the flour with the cinnamon and mix thoroughly with a hand whisk. Cover the bowl and leave to rest for at least 30 minutes. Divide the batter between small bowls, then add a different food coloring of your choice to each one.

Melt the butter in a 8–9 in (20–23 cm) frying pan; pour in enough batter to cover the bottom. Cook one side until it is golden brown, then turn it over and cook the other side. Take it out of the frying pan, and carry on making crepes until the batter is finished.

For the coconut cream: Heat the cream and coconut milk in a saucepan with half of the sugar. In another saucepan, mix the egg yolks with the remaining sugar and the cornstarch. Stir in the hot cream, put back on the heat, and cook until the mixture has thickened, stirring continuously. Take off the heat and leave to cool. Slowly fold in the whipped cream, then put the coconut cream in the refrigerator.

Alternate the different-colored crepes with the coconut cream, until the ingredients are finished. Cover the rainbow cake with whipped cream and sprinkle the grated coconut all over. Garnish with the candy balls and serve.

serves 8

> ROMANTIC CAKE

Having a Party?

INGREDIENTS

for the cake
- 3.2 oz (90 g) butter
- 7 1/2 tbsp (90 g) sugar
- 3/4 cup (75 g) sifted all-purpose flour
- 2 tbsp (15 g) unsweetened cocoa powder
- 1 tsp baking powder
- 1/3 cup (75 g) beaten egg
- 2 3/4 tbsp (40 ml) milk

for the chocolate cream
- 2 cups (500 ml) milk
- 1/2 cup (100 g) sugar
- 2 tbsp (20 g) unsweetened cocoa powder
- 3.5 oz (100 g) dark chocolate
- 6 tbsp (100 g) egg yolks
- 4 1/4 tbsp (40 g) cornstarch

for the chocolate buttercream frosting
- 21 oz (600 g) butter
- 9 1/4 cups (1.2 kg) powdered sugar
- 4 tbsp unsweetened cocoa powder

for decorating
- white fondant icing

serves 10

Hand whisk the butter, softened at room temperature, and the sugar; add the eggs one at a time, alternating them with a tablespoon of flour, then mix thoroughly. Fold in the remaining flour, cocoa powder, yeast, and finally the milk, stirring until the mixture is smooth. Pour into a 10 in (25 cm) round cake pan, buttered and floured, and bake at 350°F (180°C) for about 25 minutes. Take out of the oven and leave to cool on a cooling rack.

For the chocolate cream: In a saucepan, heat the milk with half of the sugar and the cocoa powder, until it starts bubbling. Beat the egg yolks with the remaining sugar, add the cornstarch, and mix until it becomes a batter. Slowly pour in the hot milk, put back on the heat, and cook until the cream has thickened. Take off the heat, stir in the grated chocolate, and leave to cool.

For the buttercream frosting: Cream the butter, softened at room temperature, and sugar. Add the sifted cocoa powder and mix. Put in the refrigerator.

Cut the cake into 3 layers and fill each layer with chocolate cream. Cover the whole cake with the chocolate buttercream, then put the cake in the refrigerator for at least 3 hours.

Roll out the white fondant icing and cut out shapes using a cookie cutter. Decorate the cake how you like, and serve.

> DECADENT
CHOCOLATE CAGE CAKE

INGREDIENTS

for the chocolate sponge cake
- just under 1 cup (220 g) beaten egg
- 3/4 cup (150 g) sugar
- 1 cup (130 g) cake flour
- 1/4 cup (30 g) unsweetened cocoa powder
- 1/2 vanilla pod
- pinch of salt

for the chocolate cream
- 2 cups (500 ml) milk
- 5 egg yolks
- 1/3 cup (50 g) cornstarch
- 5.3 oz (150 g) chopped dark chocolate
- 3/4 cup (150 g) sugar
- 1 vanilla pod
- 3/4 cup (200 g) whipped cream

for the rum syrup
- 6 1/4 tbsp (75 g) sugar
- 5 tbsp (75 ml) water
- 5 tbsp (75 ml) rum

you will also need
- 7 oz (200 g) sour cherries in syrup
- 3.5 oz (100 g) dark chocolate

serves 8-10

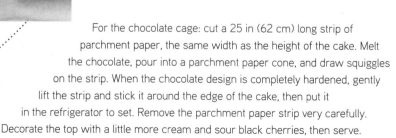

Prepare the sponge cake following the recipe in the first section of this book, but replacing the potato flour with the cocoa powder. Pour the mixture into an 8 in (20 cm) round cake pan, buttered and floured, and bake at 350°F (180°C) for about 20 minutes. Take out of the oven, turn out the cake, and leave to rest on a wire rack for at least 6 hours.

For the cream: Beat the egg yolks with the sugar and vanilla seeds; add the cornstarch and mix thoroughly. Heat the milk and immediately pour it slowly into the egg yolks. Put the cream in a saucepan and cook until it thickens, stirring continuously. Take off the heat, add the chopped chocolate, and stir until it melts completely. Cover with plastic wrap and leave to cool. Slowly fold in the whipped cream, cover, and put in the refrigerator until you need it.

For the syrup: Put the water and sugar in a saucepan and bring to a boil. Take off the heat, add the liqueur, and leave to cool.

Cut the sponge cake into three layers. Brush the first with the syrup, cover with a thin layer of cream, add a few sour cherries, and cover with the second layer of cake. Do the same with the other layers, covering the top of the cake with just cream. Put in the refrigerator and leave to set for at least 4 hours.

For the chocolate cage: cut a 25 in (62 cm) long strip of parchment paper, the same width as the height of the cake. Melt the chocolate, pour into a parchment paper cone, and draw squiggles on the strip. When the chocolate design is completely hardened, gently lift the strip and stick it around the edge of the cake, then put it in the refrigerator to set. Remove the parchment paper strip very carefully. Decorate the top with a little more cream and sour black cherries, then serve.

CREPE CAKE WITH WHITE CHOCOLATE CREAM AND MILK CHOCOLATE EGGS

Having a Party?

INGREDIENTS

for the crepes
- 2 cups (1/2 l) milk
- 3 eggs
- 1 3/4 cups (175 g) all-purpose flour
- 1/4 cup (30 g) sweetened cocoa powder
- 1-2 tbsp of butter

for the cream
- 2 cups (1/2 l) milk
- 3/4 cup (100 g) fresh cream
- 4 egg yolks
- 3/4 cup (150 g) sugar
- 5 2/3 tsp (20 g) potato flour
- 3 1/4 tbsp (20 g) all-purpose flour
- 1/2 vanilla pod
- 7 oz (200 g) white chocolate

for decorating
- 7 oz (200 g) milk chocolate eggs
- 2 oz (50 g) amaretti cookies
- 1 cup (100 g) ground hazelnuts
- 1 2/3 cups (400 ml) fresh cream
- 1/4 cup (30 g) powdered sugar

Prepare the batter for the crepes.
Break the eggs into a bowl, add the flour, cocoa powder, and milk, then whisk until the batter is smooth and lump-free.

serves 6-8

CREPE CAKE WITH WHITE CHOCOLATE CREAM AND MILK CHOCOLATE EGGS

Melt the butter in a frying pan, pour in a ladle of batter, and swirl the frying pan around so the batter coats the bottom evenly. Cook one side of the crepe, then turn it over and cook the other side. Put it to one side and continue making crepes until the batter runs out.

In a saucepan, beat the egg yolks with the sugar, flour, and potato flour. In another saucepan, bring the milk, cream, and vanilla seeds to a boil. Filter the hot liquid and pour it into the egg yolks. Stir, put back on the heat, and cook until the cream thickens. Add the chopped white chocolate and stir until it melts.

PREPARATION TIME: 1 hour   **RESTING TIME:** 2 hours

Pour the chocolate cream into a cold container and leave to cool. Slowly fold in 3/4 cup (200 g) of whipped cream from the bottom upward.

Make the cake by alternating the crepes with a layer of cream, until you have finished all the ingredients and ending with a crepe on top.

Cover with the remaining whipped cream, sweetened with the powdered sugar (leave a bit of cream for the edge), and decorate with chocolate eggs and amaretti cookies. Spread the whipped cream you put aside around the edge of the cake, then cover it with ground hazelnuts. Put in the refrigerator for at least 2 hours before serving.

› MOJITO CAKE

Having a Party?

Prepare the sponge cake following the recipe in the first section of this book, but substituting the vanilla with finely chopped mint leaves, mixed thoroughly into the batter.

Pour the batter into an 8 in (20 cm) round cake pan, previously buttered and sprinkled with flour. Bake at 350°F (180°C) for about 20 minutes. Take the sponge cake out of the oven, turn it out, and leave to rest on a wire rack for at least 6 hours.

For the syrup: Put the water and sugar in a saucepan and bring to a boil. Take off the heat, flavor with the liqueur, and stir.

For the lime cream: In a bowl, beat the eggs with the egg yolks and sugar. Mix in the butter, softened at room temperature, then add the lime zest and juice, and cook on the cooktop until thickened.

Cut the sponge cake into three layers. Put the first layer on a serving plate, brush with syrup, and cover with a layer of lime cream. Do the same with the other layers, and finish the cake with the last layer of sponge just brushed with syrup. Cover the whole cake with the remaining cream, and decorate with slices of lime and mint leaves. Leave to rest for a few hours in the refrigerator before serving.

INGREDIENTS

for the mint sponge cake
- 5 eggs
- 2/3 cup (130 g) sugar
- 1 cup (125 g) cake flour
- 2 1/3 tbsp (25 g) potato flour
- 5 mint leaves
- salt

for the syrup
- 11 1/2 tbsp (170 ml) water
- 5 tbsp (60 g) brown sugar
- 2 3/4 tbsp (40 ml) white rum

for the lime cream
- 2 limes
- 1/2 cup (100 g) castor sugar
- 2 eggs
- 2 egg yolks
- 3.5 oz (100 g) butter

for decorating
- 2 limes
- 1 sprig of mint

serves 8

❯ ROCHER CAKE

Having a Party?

for the soft caramel
- 1/2 cup (100 g) sugar
- 1/4 cup (80 g) glucose syrup
- 1 cup (120 g) cream
- 1/4 cup (60 g) sweetened condensed milk
- 1 vanilla pod
- 5.5 oz (160 g) butter
- pinch of fleur de sel

for the hazelnut praline
- just under 1 cup (250 g) peeled hazelnuts
- 1 1/3 cups (250 g) powdered sugar / • 1 vanilla pod
- pinch of fleur de sel
- a dash of water

for the mousseline cream
- 1 cup (235 ml) milk
- 3 1/4 tbsp (55 g) egg yolks
- 3 3/4 tbsp (45 g) sugar
- 2 tbsp (20 g) cornstarch
- 6 oz (175 g) hazelnut praline
- 12.3 oz (350 g) whipped butter

for the frosting
- 18.5 oz (525 g) milk chocolate
- 2/3 cup (150 g) rice oil
- 5.3 oz (150 g) chopped almonds
- Pinch of vanilla powder

for the caramelized hazelnuts
- 1 1/3 cups (200 g) peeled hazelnuts
- 1/2 cup (100 g) sugar
- 3 tsp (15 ml) water
- pinch of vanilla powder
- pinch of fleur de sel

for the syrup
- 4 tbsp (50 g) castor sugar
- 4 3/4 tbsp (70 ml) water

INGREDIENTS

for the brittle
- 5.3 oz (150 g) butter
- 3/4 cup (150 g) brown sugar
- 3/4 cup (75 g) all-purpose flour / • 3/4 cup (75 g) hazelnut flour

for the base
- 8.8 oz (250 g) milk chocolate / • 3.5 oz (100 g) hazelnut paste / • 5.3 oz (150 g) chopped almonds

for the cake
- 1/4 cup (60 g) egg white
- 7 1/2 tbsp (90 g) sugar
- 1 3/4 tbsp (25 g) beaten eggs
- 3 tbsp (50 g) egg yolks
- 2 tsp (5 g) unsweetened cocoa powder / • 6 2/3 tbsp (40 g) almond flour / • 0.5 oz (15 g) butter
- 0.5 oz (15 g) chocolate liqueur

For the brittle: Rub the butter into the brown sugar, flour, and hazelnut flour until the mixture is crumbly. Put it on a baking pan lined with parchment paper and bake at 325°F (170°C) for about 20 minutes. Take it out of the oven, leave to cool, and take it out of the pan.

For the base: Melt the milk chocolate, add it to the hazelnut paste, and mix. Add the chopped almonds and mix thoroughly. Pour the mixture into a round 7 in (18 cm) steel cake ring, spreading it into a thin layer, and leave to cool.

serves 8

❯ ❯ ❯ ❯ ❯ ❯

❯ ROCHER CAKE

For the cake: Beat the eggs and egg yolks with 5 tbsp (60 g) of sugar until they are frothy. Melt the butter and the chocolate liqueur, mixing them thoroughly. Whisk the egg whites with the remaining sugar. Pour the butter and chocolate liqueur into the egg yolk mixture, and stir thoroughly. Gradually fold in the almond flour mixed with the cocoa powder, alternating with the whipped egg whites. Pour the mixture into a round 7 in (18 cm) cake pan, buttered and floured, and bake at 350°F (180°C) for about 40 minutes. Take out of the oven, leave to cool, and turn out of the cake pan.

For the caramel: Melt the glucose syrup in a saucepan, add the sugar, and continue cooking until caramelized. In another saucepan, bring the cream, condensed milk, and vanilla seeds to a boil. Slowly pour it into the caramel, stirring continuously so as to "uncook" it. Remove from the heat, add the butter and the fleur de sel, then leave to cool.

For the praline: In a saucepan, melt the sugar and salt in 3–4 tablespoons of water, together with the vanilla seeds, until the mixture is a golden caramel color. Toast the hazelnuts in the oven and add them while still hot, stirring thoroughly. Leave the praline to cool, then chop roughly.

PREPARATION TIME: 3 hours   **COOKING TIME:** 40 min

For the cream: Beat the egg yolks with the sugar and cornstarch. Slowly pour in the hot milk, add the vanilla, stir, and put back on the heat until it thickens. Remove from the heat and leave to cool. Add the hazelnut praline, followed by the whipped butter, and stir.

For the frosting: Melt the milk chocolate. Add a drizzle of oil and emulsify, then stir in the almonds.

For the caramelized hazelnuts: In a saucepan, heat the water, sugar, vanilla, and fleur de sel to a temperature of 250°F (120°C). Add the hot toasted hazelnuts and stir. Take off the heat and leave to cool.

Put the brittle on top of the base in the cake ring, and cover with the cake; wet with a few tablespoons of syrup made with water and sugar.

Put the caramel in a pastry bag and pipe it over the top, then leave to harden. Take the cake out of the ring, cover with the frosting, and leave to set. Garnish with swirls of mousseline cream and caramelized hazelnuts, then serve.

SEDUCTION CAKE (RECIPE BY IGINIO MASSARI)

Having a Party?

Prepare the sponge cake following the recipe in the first section of this book, but substitute the vanilla with the cocoa powder, use the different quantities of egg yolks and egg whites given here, and only add the melted butter in the final step.

Divide the batter between 3 cake pans (1.5 in/4 cm high and with a diameter of 7 in/18 cm), buttered and floured, filling them 2/3 full. Bake at 350°F (180°C) for 24–25 minutes. Take out of the oven, leave to cool, and then turn out.

For the Bavarian cream: In a bowl with a semi-round bottom, hand whisk the egg yolks, rice starch, and sugar. In a saucepan, bring the milk, cream, and vanilla pod to a boil. Incorporate the two mixtures, stirring continuously with a whisk, and cook using a bain marie. The cream is ready when it starts to thicken.

INGREDIENTS

for the chocolate sponge cake
- 1/3 cup (100 g) egg yolks
- 3/4 cup (120 g) sugar
- 9 1/2 tbsp (130 g) egg white
- 1 cup (90 g) cake flour
- 2 tbsp (20 g) unsweetened cocoa powder
- 1.2 oz (35 g) melted butter

for the vanilla Bavarian cream
- 4 3/4 tbsp (80 g) egg yolks
- 1 1/3 tbsp (15 g) rice starch
- 1/4 cup (50 g) sugar
- 1 1/4 cups (150 g) light cream
- 1 vanilla pod
- 2/3 cup (150 ml) milk
- 0.1 oz (4 g) sheet gelatin
- 3/4 cup (200 g) unsweetened whipped cream

for the chocolate mousse cream
- just under 7 1/2 cups (900 g) fresh cream
- 1/2 cup (100 g) sugar
- 6 2/3 tbsp (100 ml) milk
- 10.6 oz (300 g) 70% dark chocolate
- 1/3 oz (8 g) sheet gelatin

for the orange syrup
- 1/2 cup (100 g) sugar
- 6 2/3 tbsp (100 ml) water
- 3 1/4 tbsp (50 g) orange juice
- 1/3 cup (80 g) Triple Sec

for the mirror glaze
- 1 1/4 cups (150 g) fresh cream
- 3 1/3 tbsp (50 ml) milk
- 1 3/4 tbsp (40 g) glucose syrup
- 3.5 oz (100 g) 70% dark chocolate
- 0.15 oz (5 g) sheet gelatin
- 7 1/4 tbsp (100 g) fruit gelatin

for decorating
- dark chocolate shavings
- sprigs of red currants

serves 6-8

Stir the gelatin, previously soaked in cold water, drained, and squeezed, into the hot cream, then leave to cool. When the cream reaches a temperature of 86–90°F (30–32°C), slowly add the whipped cream. Put the cake rings (0.5 in/1.5 cm high and with a diameter of 7 in/18 cm) on a baking pan lined with parchment paper. Pour the cream in and put in the freezer to stabilize.

For the mousse cream: Pour the cream, milk, and sugar into a saucepan and heat to 140°F (60°C). Remove from the heat and add the chocolate, in small pieces, and the gelatin, previously soaked in cold water, drained, and squeezed. Pour the mixture into a kitchen mixer and mix for 3 minutes at maximum speed. Put in the refrigerator at 32–40°F (0–4°C) for 24 hours, then whisk the cream in a planetary mixer or with a whisk.

For the syrup: Put the water and sugar in a saucepan and bring to a boil. Take off the heat and leave to cool, then add the orange juice and the liqueur, mixing thoroughly.

For the mirror glaze: In a saucepan, boil the cream with the milk and glucose syrup. Stir in the gelatin, previously soaked in cold water, drained, and squeezed, the fruit gelatin, and the chopped chocolate, then stir vigorously. Leave to rest in the refrigerator overnight.

Put 3 steel cake rings (1.5 in/4 cm high and with a diameter of 8 in/20 cm) on a baking pan lined with parchment paper. Cover the circumference of the rings with a strip of acetate the same height as the rings. Pour in a layer of mousse cream, level it, and cover with a layer of sponge cake dipped in syrup, cut slightly smaller than the ring. Now add a layer of Bavarian cream from the freezer. Cover with another layer of sponge cake and a layer of chocolate cream. Now add the last layer of sponge cake and put in the freezer to stabilize for about 10–12 hours.

Remove the ring and the strip of acetate from the cake, then turn upside down on a wire rack. Heat the frosting to 86–90°F/30–32 °C (using a bain marie or the microwave) and pour it over the cake, first over the edges and then over the top.
Use a spatula to remove any excess frosting. Leave it to drip and then stabilize for 3 minutes. Transfer to a plate, decorate as you like with the chocolate and sprigs of red currants, then serve.

Breakfast and Teatime

TURN YOUR OVEN ON AND GET YOUR BAKING PANS READY:
BREAKFAST AND TEATIME WILL NEVER BE THE SAME AGAIN!
NEVER SO GOOD, NEVER SO GENUINE
— BECAUSE THESE RECIPES ARE HOMEMADE, WITH
THE BEST AND FRESHEST INGREDIENTS, WITHOUT ANY
PRESERVATIVES, DYES, OR ADDITIVES OF DUBIOUS ORIGINS.
THESE DAYS, MORE THAN EVER, IT IS IMPORTANT TO
MAKE SUSTAINABLE HOUSEHOLD
CONSUMPTION CHOICES, BOTH TO
SAFEGUARD OUR HEALTH AND THE NATURAL BALANCE
IN OUR ECOSYSTEM. SHOPPING WISELY MEANS LESS
PACKAGING AND LESS WASTE, NOT TO MENTION
MORE FLAVOR, MORE WELL-BEING,
AND A BETTER QUALITY OF LIFE.
JUST THINK OF HOW MUCH TIME (AND MONEY!) YOU CAN
SAVE AND OF THE PLEASURE OF MAKING — PERHAPS WITH
YOUR KIDS OR PARTNER — A MOIST SPONGE CAKE, FLAKY
PASTRIES, FLUFFY MUFFINS, POUND CAKES, IRRESISTIBLE TARTS,
OR SCRUMPTIOUS COOKIES. THIS IS WAY BETTER THAN STANDING
IN A LINE AT THE SUPERMARKET CHECKOUT, WITH A CART FULL OF
INDUSTRIAL FOODS, RIGHT? AND LET'S NOT FORGET THOSE SWEET
AND ENVELOPING SMELLS OF OVEN-BAKED CAKES AND
COOKIES WAFTING THROUGH YOUR HOUSE!

› BALOCCHI COOKIES

For the basic sable dough: Cream the butter, softened at room temperature, with the powdered sugar. Add the eggs, the flour sifted with the salt, and the vanilla seeds. Make a loaf shape, wrap it in plastic wrap, and leave to rest overnight.

For the chocolate sable dough: Follow the basic recipe, but add the cocoa powder to the flour.

Roll out the two doughs to a thickness of 0.2 in (5 mm). Using a cookie cutter, cut out lots of small circles. Using a flat-topped pastry bag nozzle, make four small holes in each circle to make them look like buttons. Place the buttons on a baking pan lined with parchment paper, and bake at 375°F (190°C) for about 8 minutes. Take out of the oven and leave to cool.

For the ganache: Melt the chocolate using a bain marie, add the hazelnut paste, and mix thoroughly. Melt the butter and cocoa butter in a saucepan. Take the chocolate off the heat, slowly pour in the butter mixture, stir, and leave to cool. Put the mixture in the freezer and leave to cool for 5 minutes.

Whisk the mixture in a planetary mixer on high speed, until it becomes a ganache. Put it in a pastry bag and fill the cookies. Each cookie should be one half black, and one half white.

INGREDIENTS
for the regular sable dough
- 4 1/2 cups (450 g) all-purpose flour
- 10.6 oz (300 g) butter
- 1 cup (150 g) powdered sugar
- 1 3/4 tbsp (25 g) beaten egg
- 1/2 vanilla bean
- pinch of salt

for the chocolate sable dough
- 4 cups (400 g) all-purpose flour
- 7 tbsp (50 g) unsweetened cocoa powder
- 10.6 oz (300 g) butter
- 1 cup (150 g) powdered sugar
- 1 3/4 tbsp (25 g) beaten egg
- 1/2 vanilla bean
- pinch of salt

for the ganache
- 18 oz (500 g) milk chocolate
- 5.3 oz (150 g) hazelnut paste
- 1 oz (25 g) cocoa butter
- 4.2 oz (120 g) butter

makes about 40 cookies

PREPARATION TIME: 45 min   **COOKING TIME:** 8 min   155

WHOLEWHEAT SHORTBREAD COOKIES WITH ORANGE MARMALADE AND APPLES

Breakfast

For the shortbread: Rub the butter into the flour and sugar. Add a pinch of salt, the egg yolks, and the milk, then mix quickly until the dough is firm and smooth. Make it into a ball, wrap in plastic wrap, and leave to rest for at least 30 minutes in the refrigerator.

Peel the apples, remove the cores, and dice. Put them in a bowl, add a little marmalade, and stir thoroughly. Roll the shortbread out to a thickness of 0.1 in (3 mm) on a lightly floured work surface. Cut out the flowers with a cookie cutter, and put them on a baking pan lined with parchment paper. Put a teaspoon of marmalade and some diced apple on top of all of them.

Roll out the dough and cut out as many flowers as there are cookies. Using a round 0.8 in (2 cm) cookie cutter, cut out a circle in the center of each flower. Now put them on top of the other flowers and press the edges together, using a little water to help them stick. Bake at 350°F (180°C) for about 25 minutes, or until the edges are slightly golden brown. Take the cookies out of the oven and leave them to cool. Serve with a pot of aromatic mix tea.

INGREDIENTS
- 3.5 oz (100 g) diced cold butter
- 1 cup (100 g) cake flour
- 3/4 cup (100 g) wholewheat flour
- 5 tbsp (60 g) sugar
- 2 egg yolks
- 2 tbsp milk
- 2 Rennet apples or similar
- bitter orange marmalade
- salt

makes about 15 cookies

PREPARATION TIME: 45 min   **RESTING TIME:** 30 min   **COOKING TIME:** 25 min   157

› CARROT CLOUD CAKE

Breakfast

INGREDIENTS
- 2/3 cup (130 g) sugar
- 2 eggs
- 8.8 oz (250 g) peeled carrots
- 2.8 oz (80 g) butter
- 1 cup (130 g) cake flour
- 2 3/4 tbsp (30 g) potato flour
- 1 tbsp (10 g) cake yeast
- salt
- powdered sugar

Beat the eggs with the sugar and a pinch of salt until they are light and frothy. Melt the butter and leave to cool. Blend the carrots in a blender, slowly pour in the tepid melted butter, and continue to blend.

Add the carrot and butter mixture to the eggs and sugar, then mix thoroughly until smooth. Sift the flour, potato flour, and yeast into the mixture and then fold them in.

Butter and flour a half round loaf pan and pour the batter in. Bake at 350°F (180°C) for about 30–35 minutes. Take out of the oven and leave to cool. Turn the cake out onto a serving plate, sprinkle with a little powdered sugar, and serve.

TIPS
• It is important that the blended carrot becomes a pulp and that any pieces left are tiny. • For a lighter cake, it is possible to replace the granulated sugar with blended cane sugar, and to use seed oil instead of butter. • To make the cake in a classic pound cake mold, make one and a half quantities of batter. • To create decorative motifs, you can cut out strips of paper to put on the cake before sprinkling it with powdered sugar.

serves 6

PREPARATION TIME: 20 min   **COOKING TIME:** 35 min

> HONEY AND WALNUT
POUND CAKE

Finely chop just under 1 cup (200 g) of walnut kernels and put them into a bowl. Sift in the flour and yeast, add the sugar, and stir. Melt the butter in the milk over low heat. Remove from the heat and leave to cool, then stir it into the flour and walnut mixture. Put the egg into a bowl; add the honey and a pinch of salt, then beat until smooth, then add the rest of the ingredients.

Pour the batter into the pound cake mold, sprinkle the remaining walnuts on top, and bake in a preheated oven at 350°F (180°C) for about 50 minutes, using a toothpick to see if it is cooked. Take out of the oven, leave to cool, turn out of the mold, and serve.

INGREDIENTS
- 1 1/3 cup (250 g) walnut kernels
- 3 1/3 cups (300 g) cake flour
- 3.5 oz (100 g) butter
- 1/2 cup (100 g) sugar
- 1 egg
- 1 cup (2.5 dl) milk
- 2 3/4 tbsp (60 g) honey
- 1 packet of cake yeast
- salt

serves 4-6

PREPARATION TIME: 20 min   **COOKING TIME:** 50 min   161

> CHESTNUT FLOUR CAKE
WITH CARAMELIZED PEARS

Breakfast

INGREDIENTS
- 4.4 oz (125 g) butter
- 2/3 cup (125 g) sugar
- 4 eggs
- just under 1/3 cup
(125 g) chestnut flour
- 1 cup (125 g) cake flour
- 1 tbsp (10 g) cake yeast
- 1 vanilla bean
- 1 lemon
- salt

for the caramelized pears
- 3 Abate Fetel pears or
similar
- 3 tbsp brown sugar
- 3 tbsp rum

Peel the pears, cut them in half, and remove
the cores. Cut each half diagonally into a fan, then
put them in a non-stick pan with the sugar
and rum. Put on the cooktop and cook until
the liquid has absorbed and the pears are
caramelized. Turn off and leave to cool.

With a whisk, mix the butter, softened at room
temperature, with the sugar, a pinch of salt,
and the vanilla seeds. Lightly beat the eggs
and add them alternately to the mixture with
the flours, previously sifted with the yeast.
Fragrance with the lemon zest and pour
into a round 8 in (20 cm) cake pan, buttered
and floured.

Put the caramelized pears on top of the cake
and bake at 350°F (180°C) for about 45–50 minutes.
Take out of the oven and leave to cool. Gently turn
the cake out onto a cake rack and serve.

serves 6

PREPARATION TIME: 30 min   **COOKING TIME:** 50 min

> APPLE AND BLUEBERRY CAKE

Soak the blueberries in the rum. Peel the apples, remove the cores, and cut into slices, every now and then squeezing lemon juice over them to prevent them from turning brown. Add a pinch of cinnamon and mix.

Sift the flour, potato flour, and yeast into a bowl, then make a well in the middle. Pour the melted butter into the well, then add the sugar, milk, eggs, the zest of 1/2 a lemon, the vanilla seeds, and a pinch of salt; mix thoroughly. Add 2/3 of the blueberries, squeezed thoroughly, and stir.

Pour the batter into a round 9 in (23 cm) cake pan, buttered and floured. Add the apples, letting them sink into the batter, and then the remaining blueberries. Bake at 350°F (180°C) for about 45 minutes (use a toothpick to see if it is cooked, and if necessary, cook for another 5–10 minutes). Take the cake out of the oven and leave it to cool. Turn it out onto a cake rack and leave to cool completely. It is now ready to serve.

INGREDIENTS

- 28 oz (800 g) Golden Delicious apples
- 2 cups (180 g) cake flour
- 3/4 cup (120 g) sugar
- 4 2/3 tbsp (50 g) potato flour
- 3.5 oz (100 g) melted butter
- 2 eggs
- 3 1/3 tbsp (50 ml) milk
- 2/3 cup (100 g) dried blueberries
- 1 tbsp (10 g) cake yeast
- 1/2 lemon
- 1/2 vanilla pod
- 4 tbsp rum
- ground cinnamon
- salt

serves 8-10

PREPARATION TIME: 30 min   **COOKING TIME:** 50 min

❯ APRICOT AND RICOTTA BRAID

Breakfast

INGREDIENTS
- 3 cups (300 g) all-purpose flour
- 2 eggs
- 2 tsp (5 g) brewer's yeast
- 1/2 cup (1.25 dl) milk
- 1.7 oz (50 g) butter
- 3 1/3 tbsp (40 g) sugar
- 1 vanilla bean

for the filling
- 10.5 oz (300 g) ricotta cheese
- 2/3 cup (100 g) dried apricots
- 1/4 cup (50 g) sugar
- 1 egg
- 3 level tbsp cornstarch
- 2 tbsp dried breadcrumbs

Dilute the yeast in warm milk with 1 tsp of sugar and 2 tbsp of flour. Cover and leave to rise for about half an hour, or until the mixture doubles in volume.

Melt the butter over low heat and pour it into a bowl. Add 1 egg, the remaining sugar, and the vanilla seeds. Add the leavened mixture and the remaining flour, then mix vigorously until the dough is firm and smooth. Make it into a ball, cover with a clean cloth, and leave to rise for half an hour.

For the filling: Mix the ricotta cheese with the sugar, egg, and cornstarch until creamy. Chop the apricots into small pieces, add them to the cream, and mix thoroughly.

Roll out the dough into a thin rectangle. Score the rectangle lengthwise into three equal parts: sprinkle the central part with the breadcrumbs and cover with the filling. Cut the other two parts into horizontal strips (without detaching them from the central part), then braid the right and left strips over the filling until it is covered.

Seal the edges of the braid, transfer it to a baking pan lined with parchment paper, and brush it with the remaining beaten egg. Put in a preheated oven at 350°F (180°C) and bake for about 35 minutes. Take it out of the oven, leave to cool, and serve.

serves 6-8

> STRAWBERRY AND BLACK PEPPER TART

Teatime

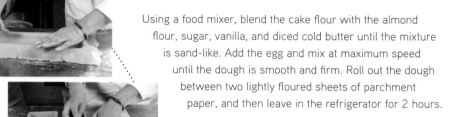

INGREDIENTS
- 2 3/4 cups (245 g) cake flour
- 1/3 cup (35 g) almond flour
- 4.5 oz (130 g) cold salted butter
- 1 large egg
- 2/3 cup (85 g) powdered sugar
- 1 tsp vanilla extract
- 1 egg white

for the filling
- 1 lb 4 oz (500 g) strawberries
- 1 lemon
- 6 mint leaves
- pinch of black pepper
- 3 Granny Smith apples
- 6 tbsp (70 g) sugar
- 1/3 oz (8 g) sheet gelatin

for decorating
- mixed berries

Using a food mixer, blend the cake flour with the almond flour, sugar, vanilla, and diced cold butter until the mixture is sand-like. Add the egg and mix at maximum speed until the dough is smooth and firm. Roll out the dough between two lightly floured sheets of parchment paper, and then leave in the refrigerator for 2 hours.

Carefully put the pastry in a shallow cake pan, pressing the bottom and edges onto the pan. Cut off any excess pastry with a knife, then put it back in the refrigerator for 30–40 minutes.

Pierce the base with a fork, cover with a sheet of parchment paper and ceramic pie beans, and bake at 350°F (180°C) for 15–20 minutes. Take out of the oven, remove the paper and beans, brush with egg white, and cook for a further 5 minutes. Take out of the oven and leave to cool.

For the filling: Soak the gelatin in iced water. Blend the strawberries with half of the lemon juice, and pass the puree through a medium-mesh strainer. Peel the apples, remove the cores, and dice them. Put them into a glass bowl and drizzle with the remaining lemon juice. Cover with plastic wrap and cook in the microwave at maximum power for about 5 minutes.

Put the diced apples into a mixer and blend them. Add the drained and well-squeezed gelatin, the strawberry puree, sugar, mint leaves, and pepper, then mix thoroughly. As soon as the mixture has cooled, pour it onto the pastry base and put in the refrigerator for about 2 hours. Decorate with mixed berries and serve.

serves 8

› APPLE ROSE TART

INGREDIENTS
for the sweet shortcrust pastry
- 4.4 oz (125 g) butter
- 7 1/2 tbsp (90 g) castor sugar
- 2 egg yolks
- 2 1/4 cups (200 g) cake flour
- 1 Bourbon vanilla pod
- 1 lemon
- salt

for the custard
- 2 cups (500 ml) milk
- 3/4 cup (150 g) sugar
- 6 egg yolks
- 2 2/3 tbsp (25 g) cornstarch
- 2 tbsp (20 g) rice starch
- 1 oz (30 g) butter
- 1 lemon
- 1 vanilla bean
- ground cinnamon
- salt

for the roses
- 8 large red apples (not mealy)
- 4 1/4 cups (1 l) water
- 2 1/3 cups (450 g) sugar
- 1 1/2 lemons

Prepare the sweet shortcrust pastry following the recipe on page 24, but substituting the powdered sugar with castor sugar. Make into a ball, wrap in plastic wrap, and leave to rest in the refrigerator for one hour.

serves 10

❯ APPLE ROSE TART

For the cream: In a saucepan, bring the milk to a boil with a pinch of salt, the lemon zest, a pinch of cinnamon, and half of the vanilla pod. In another pan, beat the egg yolks with the sugar until frothy; add the sifted cornstarch and rice starch, then mix thoroughly. Filter the boiling milk and stir in slowly, then put back on the heat and cook until the cream has thickened.

Pour the cream into an oven pan, leave it to cool slightly (to about 120°F/50°C), and then add the diced butter. Cover with plastic wrap and leave to cool in the refrigerator for at least 3 hours.

Roll out the pastry on a floured work surface, to a thickness of about 0.2 in (5 mm). Line a round 10 in (26 cm) cake pan, buttered and floured, and pierce the bottom with a fork. Cover with a sheet of parchment paper and baking beans, and bake at 350°F (180°C) for about 15 minutes. Remove the paper and beans, and cook for another 10–12 minutes. Take the tart out of the oven and leave to cool.

172   **PREPARATION TIME:** 1 hour   **RESTING TIME:** 60 min   **COOKING TIME:** 45 min

For the roses: Wash the apples, remove the cores, and use a mandoline to cut them into slices with a thickness of about 0.1 in (3 mm). Put them into a bowl with cold water mixed with the juice of 1/2 a lemon. Pour the water, sugar, and lemon juice into a saucepan, and bring to a boil. Add the slices of apple and leave to cook for about 3 minutes. Drain them with a slotted spoon, put them on a clean cloth, and leave them to cool.

Put the cream into the pastry crust and level with a spatula. Take 5 slices of the now cold apple and put them horizontally onto the work surface, overlapping them slightly. Roll them around each other to make the rose and then put it on top of the cream. Make the rest of the roses in the same way, arranging them from the outside inward until the top of the tart is completely covered. It is now ready to serve.

TIPS
• You can also flavor the cream with orange zest by simply putting it into the milk while it is boiling. • After taking the beans out of the oven and leaving them to cool, you can keep them in a bag to use again. • If you don't have a mandoline or a slicer, you can cut the apples with a knife. • If you want to keep the tart for 3 days, brush the apple roses with a very light film of gelatin and leave them in the refrigerator.

› CITRUS-SCENTED SHORTBREAD COOKIES

Teatime

INGREDIENTS
- just under 4 1/2 cups (400 g) cake flour
- 8 oz (230 g) butter
- 2/3 cup (130 g) powdered sugar
- 4 egg yolks
- 2 eggs
- 1 orange
- 1 lemon
- 1 tsp milk
- salt
- pearl sugar

Cream the butter, softened at room temperature, with the sugar until light and frothy. Add the egg yolks, one at a time, and an egg, then fragrance with the citrus zests.

Add the flour and a pinch of salt, then mix quickly until the dough is smooth and firm. Make it into a ball, wrap in plastic wrap, and leave to rest in the refrigerator for about 30 minutes.

Roll out the dough on a lightly floured pastry board, to a thickness of about 0.2 in (5 mm). Brush the pastry with the remaining egg, previously beaten with 1 tsp milk, then cut out lots of rhombus-shaped cookies with a fluted pastry wheel.

Sprinkle the cookies with a little pearl sugar, arrange them on a baking pan lined with parchment paper, and bake in a preheated oven at 325°F (170°C) for about 15 minutes. Take out of the oven, leave to cool on a wire rack, and serve.

makes about 40 shortbread cookies

PREPARATION TIME: 20 min   **RESTING TIME:** 30 min   **COOKING TIME:** 15 min

> RASPBERRY AND MILK
CREAM ROLLS

INGREDIENTS

for the milk cream
- 6 oz (170 g) white chocolate
- 0.1 oz (3 g) sheet gelatin
- 6 2/3 tbsp (100 ml) milk
- 1 2/3 cups (200 g) fresh cream

for the chocolate cake
- 9 1/2 tbsp (130 g) egg whites
- 7 tbsp (85 g) sugar
- 5 2/3 tbsp (95 g) egg yolk
- 1/3 cup (40 g) unsweetened cocoa powder

for decorating
- 5 1/4 oz (150 g) fresh raspberries

For the cream: Put the gelatin sheets to soak in cold water and ice. Heat the milk in a saucepan, and add the roughly chopped chocolate when it comes to a boil. Stir in the drained and well-squeezed gelatin sheets, and emulsify with a hand mixer until creamy.

Slowly pour in the cold fresh cream and mix thoroughly. Cover with plastic wrap and put in the refrigerator overnight.

For the cake: Whisk the egg whites with the sugar and egg yolks; when it is nicely whipped, stir in the sifted cocoa powder with a whisk from the bottom upward. Spread the mixture out on a baking pan lined with parchment paper, to a thickness of about 0.2 in (5 mm). Bake at 350°F (180°C) for 6 minutes (be careful it doesn't dry out). Take out of the oven and leave to cool.

Cover the cake with the milk cream and then carefully roll it up. Cut the ends to form a trunk shape. Blend the raspberries, keeping a few for decorating, and pass it through a strainer. Pour a little raspberry cream on the plates and put two half rolls on top. Garnish with the remaining raspberries and serve.

serves 6-8

PREPARATION TIME: 45 min   **COOKING TIME:** 6 min

WHITE CHOCOLATE, LIME, AND POPPY SEED SQUARES

Teatime

INGREDIENTS
- 2 eggs
- 1/2 cup (100 g) sugar
- 1/4 cup (60 g) seed oil
- 6 2/3 tbsp (100 ml) lime juice (about 4 limes)
- 1 cup (100 g) cake flour
- 2 tsp cake yeast
- 4 tbsp poppy seeds
- 7 oz (200 g) white chocolate

Line a square 7 in (18 cm) cake pan with a sheet of parchment paper. Using an electric hand mixer, whisk the eggs with the sugar until light and frothy. Slowly pour in the oil and the lime juice, and continue to whisk. Gradually fold in the sifted flour and yeast, then add the poppy seeds.

Pour the batter into the cake pan and bake at 350°F (180°C) for about 35 minutes (use a toothpick to see if it is cooked). Take the cake out of the oven and leave to cool completely.

Melt the chocolate using a bain marie, pour it over the cake, making sure all the surfaces are covered. Put in the refrigerator to set, then cut into squares. Serve with a pot of mint tea.

makes 16 squares

› CHOCOLATE AND ALMOND PHYLLO CIGARS

Teatime

Roughly chop the chocolate and put it in a food mixer. Add the almonds and sugar, and pulse until the mixture is a powder.

Cut the sheets of phyllo dough in half. Brush both sheets with melted butter, then coat one of the two shorter sides of the rectangle with the chocolate and almond powder. Fold the edges lengthwise and roll up into the shape of a cigar. Continue until you have finished all the ingredients.

Put the cigars onto a baking pan lined with parchment paper, and bake at 400°F (200°C) for about 15 minutes, or until they are golden brown. Take the cigars out of the oven, leave to cool, and serve.

INGREDIENTS
- 3.5 oz (100 g) dark chocolate
- 2/3 cup (100 g) unshelled almonds
- 1/2 cup (100 g) sugar
- 8 sheets of phyllo dough
- 1.7 oz (50 g) melted butter

makes 16 cigars

PREPARATION TIME: 20 min   **COOKING TIME:** 15 min

❯ TIRAMISU VOL-AU-VENTS

Teatime

INGREDIENTS
- 8 oz (250 g)
puff pastry
- 0.7 oz (20 g) melted
butter
- powdered sugar
- milk

for the cream
- 1/4 cup (50 g) sugar
- 3 egg yolks
- 8 oz (250 g)
mascarpone
- 1 cold espresso coffee

for decorating
- 5 coffee beans
- unsweetened cocoa
powder

Roll out the puff pastry and cut out 15 circles
with a cookie cutter. Put 5 circles on a baking pan
lined with parchment paper and brush them
with a drop of milk. Using a smaller cookie
cutter, cut out a hole in the middle of the
remaining 10 circles. Brush them with milk
and put two on top of each of the 5 circles.

Use the butter to brush the top of the
vol-au-vents. Sprinkle with a little powdered
sugar and bake at 400°F (200°C) for about
20 minutes, or until they are golden brown. Take
out of the oven and leave to cool completely.

Beat the egg yolks with the sugar until they are
light and frothy. Fold in the mascarpone. Put
the cream in a pastry bag with a star nozzle. Brush
the bottom of the vol-au-vents with the coffee
and fill them all with cream. Sprinkle with a pinch
of cocoa powder, garnish with a coffee bean, and serve.

makes 5 vol-au-vents

PREPARATION TIME: 20 min   **COOKING TIME:** 20 min

› WAFFLES WITH WHITE CHOCOLATE CREAM AND RASPBERRIES

Teatime

For the cream: Beat the egg yolks with the sugar until they are light and frothy. Heat the fresh cream in a saucepan, add the eggs, stir, and bring to a temperature of 185°F (85°C). Add the chopped chocolate and emulsify with an immersion blender. Put in the refrigerator and leave to rest for at least 4 hours.

Cream the butter, softened at room temperature, with an electric hand mixer until it is frothy. Add the sugar, milk, and egg yolks, then mix thoroughly. Continue whisking while slowly adding the sifted flour and yeast. Then add the whipped egg whites and a pinch of salt, folding them in gently from the bottom upward.

Heat a waffle maker and pour in a small amount of batter. Close the lid and cook for a few minutes, until it is golden brown and crispy. Remove and continue making the waffles until the batter is finished.

Put the waffles on individual plates and top with a little white chocolate cream. Garnish with a few raspberries, sprinkle with a little powdered sugar, and serve.

INGREDIENTS
- 3.5 oz (100 g) butter
- 1/2 cup (100 g) sugar
- 3 egg whites
- 2 1/2 cups (250 g) all-purpose flour
- 2 tsp (5 g) cake yeast
- 2/3 cup (1.6 dl) milk
- salt

for the white chocolate cream
- 8.8 oz (250 g) white chocolate
- 1 2/3 cups (200 g) fresh cream
- 3 tbsp (50 g) egg yolks
- 1 2/3 tbsp (20 g) sugar

for decorating
- raspberries
- powdered sugar

serves 4-6

PREPARATION TIME: 40 min   **COOKING TIME:** 20 min

Traditional Holidays

With a Modern Touch

^

Holidays are the times we all look for SPECIAL RECIPES to amaze our friends and relatives with, and also recipes that are CHALLENGING AND DARING. Something much more elaborate than usual, so we can practice our skills and have the sheer pleasure of finding out what we are truly capable of. In this section, you will find all this and much more, and not only recipes for Christmas — like the Gingerbread Tree, Spiced Christmas Cake, and Panforte — but for special occasions in general. You can try your hand at Chocolate and Cinnamon Fritter Knots for Carnival; Chili Caprese Cake, Chocolate Heart with Toffee Sauce, or Red Velvet cake for Valentine's Day; Mini Glazed Colombas and Neapolitan Pastiera for Easter; and Witch Hats, Spider Pumpkin Cupcakes, or Bat Cupcakes for Halloween. FUN to make, YUMMY to eat — they are the PERFECT HOMEMADE GIFT. Just browse through the pages and choose the right one for you. Are you ready to MAKE SOME MIND-BLOWING DESSERTS?

> CHOCOLATE AND CINNAMON FRITTER KNOTS WITH VANILLA CREAM

Carnival

INGREDIENTS
• 2 2/3 cups (350 g) all-purpose flour
• 2 tbsp (15 g) unsweetened cocoa powder
• 2 large eggs
• 3 tbsp (40 g) grapeseed or corn oil
• 3 tbsp (25 g) powdered sugar
• 1/4 cup (60 ml) milk
• 1 tsp cake yeast
• ground cinnamon
• peanut oil
• powdered sugar

for the vanilla cream
• 1 2/3 cups (400 ml) milk
• 3 1/4 tbsp (30 g) cornstarch or tapioca
• 4 1/4 tsp (30 g) maple syrup or honey
• 1 tsp vanilla powder

serves 10

Sift the flour into a bowl. Add the yeast, cocoa powder, 1 tbsp of cinnamon, sugar, oil, and the eggs, then mix the ingredients with a fork. Slowly pour the milk in and mix again until you have a soft dough.

Put the dough on a work surface and knead for at least 2–3 minutes, making a smooth loaf shape. Wrap in plastic wrap and leave to rest in a cool place for at least one hour.

With a rolling pin, roll out the dough on sheets of parchment paper sprinkled with a little cocoa powder. Fold it in half and roll out again. Repeat at least 3–4 times (the more times you roll and fold the dough, the more air bubbles you remove: this will make the pastry fritter light and crispy). Roll out to a thin sheet of about 0.03 in (1 mm). Using a pastry wheel, cut out rectangle strips measuring about 1 x 14 in (3 x 35 cm), and tie a loose knot in them.

For the vanilla cream: In a saucepan, dissolve the cornstarch and the vanilla in the milk. Cook over low heat, stirring regularly, until the cream has thickened. Take off the heat, add the maple syrup, and stir thoroughly. Put to one side and leave to cool.

Fry a few pastry fritters at a time in very hot seed oil, cooking them on both sides until they are brown. Drain and dry on a paper towel. Sprinkle with powdered sugar (as little or as much as you like), and serve with the vanilla cream.

PREPARATION TIME: 40 min   **RESTING TIME: 60 min**   **COOKING TIME: 20 min**

› PHYLLO PARCELS WITH CHOCOLATE ALMOND PASTE AND BANANAS

Carnival

Make the cream the day before. In a saucepan, dissolve the tapioca, cocoa powder, and vanilla in the almond milk. Cook over low heat, stirring regularly, until the cream has thickened. Take off the heat, add the dark chocolate and grated almond paste, then mix thoroughly. Leave to cool and leave in the refrigerator overnight.

Cut the sheets of phyllo dough into rectangles measuring about 7 x 5 in (18 x 12 cm). Brush them with a little oil and put one on top of another, two sheets for each parcel. Put 4 slices of banana and 1 heaping teaspoon of chocolate cream in the middle, then fold in the sides to make parcels. Wet your fingers with water and fold over the ends.

Put the parcels on a baking pan lined with parchment paper and bake at 350°F (180°C) for about 10 minutes, or until golden brown. Take out of the oven and put on a serving plate. Cover with 1 tsp of cream, garnish with rainbow sprinkles, and serve.

INGREDIENTS
- 20 sheets of phyllo dough
- 2 bananas
- grapeseed or corn oil

for the chocolate cream
- 1 1/4 cups (300 ml) almond milk
- 2.8 oz (80 g) 60% dark chocolate
- 2.8 oz (80 g) almond paste
- 3 1/4 tbsp (30 g) tapioca or cornstarch
- 1 1/2 tbsp (10 g) unsweetened cocoa powder
- 1/2 tsp vanilla powder

for decorating
- rainbow sprinkles

serves 10

› CHILI CAPRESE CAKE

Valentine's Day

Melt the chocolate using a bain marie and leave it to cool. In the meantime, cream the butter, softened at room temperature, with the sugar. Add the egg yolks, one at a time, almonds, 1 tsp of chili powder, and the still warm melted chocolate, then mix thoroughly. Whisk the egg whites until they are stiff and fold a few tablespoonfuls into the batter to soften it. Carefully add the remaining egg whites, folding them in with a spatula from the bottom upward.

Pour the batter into a round 8 in (20 cm) cake pan, buttered and lined with parchment paper. Bake at 325°F (170°C) for about one hour (use a toothpick to see if it is cooked, and if necessary, cook for another 10 minutes).

Take the cake out of the oven and leave to rest for 20 minutes. Turn it out onto a cake rack and leave to cool completely. Sprinkle generously with powdered sugar and serve.

INGREDIENTS
for the base
- 1 1/2 cup (240 g) chopped almonds
- 7 oz (200 g) dark chocolate
- 6.5 oz (185 g) butter
- 3/4 cup (160 g) sugar
- 4 eggs
- chili powder
- powdered sugar

serves 6-8

PREPARATION TIME: 20 min   **RESTING TIME:** 20 min   **COOKING TIME:** 60 min   193

› CHOCOLATE HEART WITH TOFFEE SAUCE

Valentine's Day

INGREDIENTS

for the base
- 3 2/3 tbsp (50 g) egg whites
- 6 tbsp (50 g) powdered sugar
- 1.7 oz (50 g) butter
- 7 tbsp (40 g) cake flour
- 1.4 oz (40 g) grated dark chocolate

for the chocolate mousse
- 7 oz (200 g) dark chocolate
- 1 1/4 cups (150 g) fresh light cream
- 1 2/3 cups (200 g) fresh semi-whipped cream

for the toffee sauce
- 1/2 cup (100 g) sugar
- 3/4 cup (100 g) fresh light cream
- 0.7 oz (20 g) butter

In a bowl, cream the butter, softened at room temperature, with the powdered sugar until frothy. Add the grated chocolate, mix thoroughly, then add the flour alternating with the egg whites. Mix thoroughly. Pour the batter into a buttered and floured heart-shaped springform cake pan, with a diameter of 6 in (15 cm). Bake at 350°F (180°C) for about 10 minutes, then take out of the oven and leave to cool.

For the mousse: Finely chop the chocolate and put it in a bowl. Heat the cream in a saucepan, take off the heat as soon as it comes to a boil, and add the chocolate. Stir until smooth and velvety, then leave to cool. Gently fold in the semi-whipped cream. Line the edge of the heart-shaped cake pan with a strip of acetate. Cover the base of the cake with the mousse, level, and put in the freezer for one hour.

For the toffee sauce: Dissolve the sugar in a thick-bottomed pan and take off the heat when it has turned dark amber. Heat the fresh cream in another saucepan. Take off the heat as soon as it starts to boil, then slowly pour it into the caramel. Stir in the butter, softened at room temperature, and leave to cool. Put in the refrigerator until you need it.

Take the cake out of the freezer and carefully remove it from the cake pan. Put the toffee sauce into a paper cone and pipe a lattice design on top of the cake. It is now ready to serve.

serves 4

PREPARATION TIME: 40 min   **COOLING TIME:** 60 min   **COOKING TIME:** 10 min

> RED VELVET

INGREDIENTS
- 3 cups (270 g) cake flour
- 3.5 oz (100 g) butter
- 1 1/3 cups (250 g) castor sugar
- 1 tbsp unsweetened cocoa powder
- 2 cups (250 g) buttermilk
- 3 eggs
- 1 tsp white vinegar
- 1 tbsp vanilla extract
- 1 tsp cake yeast
- 1/2 tsp baking soda
- 1/2 tsp salt
- 1 tbsp red food coloring gel

for the buttermilk
- 4 cups (500 g) fresh cream

for the mascarpone cream
- 2 cups (250 g) fresh cream
- 8 oz (250 g) mascarpone
- 6 tbsp (50 g) powdered sugar
- 1 tsp vanilla extract

for decorating
- red and pink sugar cake decorations

serves 6-8

For the buttermilk: Whisk the cream with a hand mixer for at least 20 minutes, until the liquid separates from the fat, then filter and put to one side. In a bowl, cream the butter, softened at room temperature, with the sugar until light and frothy. Add the eggs one at a time, gently stirring after each one. Sift the flour with the cocoa powder, yeast, and baking soda, and add it to the mixture a little at a time, alternating with the buttermilk. Add the vinegar, vanilla extract, salt, and the food coloring, then mix thoroughly (you can add more food coloring to get the color you want).

Pour the batter into a round 7 in (18 cm) cake pan with high sides, buttered and floured. Bake at 325°F (170°C) for about 60 minutes (use a toothpick to see if it is cooked before taking it out of the oven). Take out of the oven, leave the cake to cool for at least 15 minutes, then turn it out onto a wire rack to cool completely.

For the cream: In a bowl, mix the cream, powdered sugar, and vanilla extract. Add the mascarpone, stirring first with a spatula, and then whisking with an electric hand mixer until the mixture is frothy.

Cut the cake into 4 equal layers and build the cake on a serving plate, filling the layers with the mascarpone cream. Cover the whole cake with the mascarpone cream, and then put dollops around the top edge of the cake. Decorate how you like with the sugar cake decorations and serve.

PREPARATION TIME: 40 min   **COOKING TIME:** 60 min

› MINI GLAZED COLOMBAS

INGREDIENTS
- 3 3/4 cup (375 g) all-purpose flour
- 2/3 cup (150 ml) milk
- 0.7 oz (20 g) butter
- 2 1/2 tbsp (30 g) castor sugar
- 1 1/2 tbsp (15 g) brewer's yeast
- 2.8 oz (80 g) dark chocolate chips
- 6 1/3 tbsp (50 g) diced candied orange peel
- 1 tsp (5 g) salt
- 2 small eggs

for the glaze
- 6 1/4 tbsp (75 g) sugar
- 1/4 cup (25 g) almond flour
- 1 egg white

for decorating
- about 2/3 cup (100 g) whole, unpeeled almonds
- about 3.5 oz (100 g) pearl sugar
- 2 tbsp powdered sugar
- fabric ribbon

Dissolve the yeast in the milk. Put the flour into a bowl, add the sugar, the milk with the yeast, and the eggs, then start kneading. Add the salt and continue kneading. Finally, add the butter and knead until the dough is smooth and firm.

Make it into a loaf shape, wrap in plastic wrap, and leave to rise at a temperature of 80°F (26°C) until it has doubled in size. Add the chocolate chips and pieces of candied orange peel, then knead again gently.

Divide the dough into balls weighing 4 oz (100 g) each, and put them in mini dove-shaped cupcake liners. Cover and leave them to rise until they have doubled in volume.

For the glaze: Mix the sugar with the almond flour. Add the egg white and stir until you have a thick cream. Spread the surface of the colombas with the glaze, and sprinkle with whole almonds, pearl sugar, and powdered sugar. Bake at 350°F (180°C) for about 15–20 minutes.

Once cooked, take out of the oven and leave to cool. Garnish with a fabric ribbon and serve.

makes about 10 mini colombas

PREPARATION TIME: 30 min   **COOKING TIME:** 20 min

› NEAPOLITAN PASTIERA

Easter

INGREDIENTS
for the sweet shortcrust pastry
- 4 cups (350 g) cake flour
- 4.5 oz (130 g) butter
- 2 eggs
- 2/3 cup (130 g) sugar
- pinch of salt
- zest of 1/2 grated lemon

for the filling
- 18 oz (500 g) sheep ricotta cheese
- 14 oz (400 g) whole wheat berries (grano cotto)
- 6 2/3 tbsp (100 ml) milk
- 1 3/4 cup (330 g) sugar
- 1-2 tbsp of butter
- 4 eggs
- 2 egg yolks
- 3/4 cup (100 g) candied orange peel
- ground cinnamon
- 2 tsp vanilla extract
- 1 orange
- 1 lemon
- 1 tube of orange blossom essence
- salt

Make the sweet shortcrust pastry the day before. Make a well in the flour, add the other ingredients, and mix quickly until you have a smooth, firm dough. Make into a ball, wrap in plastic wrap, and put in the refrigerator. A few hours before you start preparing the filling, put the ricotta cheese in a sifter to drip, and put it in the refrigerator.

Put the whole wheat berries in a pan and add the milk, butter, a pinch of salt, and the grated citrus zests.

serves 10

> NEAPOLITAN PASTIERA

Cook for about 30 minutes, stirring regularly. Take off the heat and leave to cool at room temperature.

Pass the ricotta cheese through a strainer, put it in a bowl, and mix with the sugar. Add the lightly beaten eggs and egg yolks, the wheat cream, and the diced candied orange peel. Sprinkle with a little cinnamon, then add the vanilla extract and the orange blossom essence.

PREPARATION TIME: 60 min   **COOKING TIME:** 100 min

Roll out the sweet shortcrust pastry with a rolling pin, to a thickness of about 0.2 in (5 mm). Line a round 10 in (24 cm) pie pan, buttered and floured. Pour the filling in and create a lattice design on the top with strips of sweet shortcrust pastry. Bake at 325°F (170°C) for about one hour and 40 minutes.

Take out of the oven, leave to cool, turn out on a serving plate, and serve.

› WITCH HATS

Halloween

INGREDIENTS
- 1 2/3 cups (150 g) cake flour
- 1/4 cup (25 g) unsweetened cocoa powder
- 9 1/4 tbsp (75 g) vanilla powdered sugar
- 4.4 oz (125 g) butter
- 1 egg yolk
- salt

for the chocolate ganache
- 9 1/4 tbsp (70 g) fresh cream
- 5.3 oz (150 g) dark chocolate

you will also need
- powdered sugar
- 3.5 oz (100 g) orange fondant icing
- apricot gelatin

In a bowl, cream the room temperature butter with the sugar and a pinch of salt; add the egg yolk and mix thoroughly. Fold in the flour sifted with the cocoa powder and stir. Put the mixture on a work surface and knead until soft and smooth. Make into a ball, wrap in plastic wrap, and leave in the refrigerator for one hour.

For the ganache: Finely chop the chocolate and put it in a bowl. Pour the cream into a saucepan and heat. When it starts boiling, pour it over the chocolate and leave for about 1 minute, then stir until smooth and velvety. Leave to cool.

Roll out the dough to a thickness of about 0.2 in (5 mm). Using a round 2.5 in (7 cm) cookie cutter, cut out circles and arrange them on a baking pan lined with parchment paper. Bake at 350°F (180°C) for about 10 minutes, then take out of the oven and leave to cool on a cake rack.

Sprinkle the work surface with powdered sugar. Roll out the fondant icing into a thin sheet and cut out lots of circles with a round 1.5 in (4 cm) cooker cutter. Lightly brush each circle with the apricot gelatin and stick them onto the cookies. Put the ganache in a pastry bag with a flat-topped nozzle, and pipe long pointy dollops in the center of the fondant icing.

Take to the table and serve.

makes about 25 oz (700 g) of cookies

› SPIDER PUMPKIN CUPCAKES

Halloween

Dice the pumpkin, put it in a kitchen mixer, add the milk and oil, and blend to a puree. Whisk the egg whites with a pinch of salt until they are stiff. Beat the egg yolks with the sugar, add the pumpkin puree, vanilla extract, and orange zest, and mix thoroughly.

Add the flour sifted with the yeast and the chopped almonds. Slowly fold in the whipped egg whites from the bottom upward. Fill the cups halfway with the batter, and bake at 350°F (180°C) for about 20 minutes. Take out of the oven and leave to cool.

Cut the licorice rings into pieces 2–3 in (5–8 cm) long, and put 8 "legs" on top of each cupcake. Brush the top of the cupcakes with gelatin, sprinkle with chocolate shavings, then decorate with the candy-coated fennel seeds. Leave to cool completely before serving.

INGREDIENTS
- 4.4 oz (125 g) raw, uncooked pumpkin
- 3 2/3 tbsp (50 ml) seed oil
- 2 3/4 tbsp (40 ml) milk
- 3/4 cup (120 g) sugar
- 4 eggs
- 1/4 tbsp (140 g) cake flour
- 1/3 cup (60 g) finely chopped almonds
- 2 1/2 tsp (8 g) cake yeast
- zest of 1 orange
- 1 tsp vanilla extract
- salt

for decorating
- chocolate shavings
- licorice rings
- candy-coated fennel seeds
- apricot gelatin

makes about 12 cupcakes

PREPARATION TIME: 30 min   **COOKING TIME:** 20 min

› HALLOWEEN BATS

INGREDIENTS

- 1/4 tbsp (140 g) cake flour
- 1 cup (180 g) sugar
- 1/2 cup (120 ml) milk
- 1/3 cup (80 ml) seed oil
- 2 tbsp (20 g) unsweetened cocoa powder
- 2 eggs
- just under 2 tsp (6 g) cake yeast
- 1 tsp vanilla extract

for the chocolate ganache
- 1 2/3 cups (200 g) fresh cream
- 7 oz (200 g) dark chocolate

for decorating
- 1.7 oz (50 g) fondant icing
- chocolate drops
- 12 chocolate shortbread cookies
- apricot gelatin

Put the eggs and sugar into a bowl, and mix with an electric hand mixer until they are light and frothy. Add the oil, milk, and vanilla extract, and mix again. Fold in the flour sifted with the cocoa powder and yeast, then fill the cups halfway with the batter. Bake at 325°F (170°C) for about 20 minutes. Take out of the oven and leave to cool.

For the ganache: Finely chop the chocolate and put it in a bowl. Pour the cream into a saucepan and heat. When it starts boiling, pour it over the chocolate and leave for about 1 minute, then stir until smooth and velvety. Leave to cool, then cover with plastic wrap and put in the fridge for 2 hours.

Mix the ganache with an electric hand mixer for about 5 minutes, then put it in a pastry bag and pipe it onto the top of the cupcakes. Break the chocolate shortbread cookies in half and arrange them like wings. For the eyes, make small balls of fondant icing and flatten them slightly with your finger. Use a little gelatin to stick a chocolate drop in the middle of each eyeball. Leave to set completely before serving.

makes about 12 cupcakes

PREPARATION TIME: 40 min   **COOKING TIME:** 20 min

> GINGERBREAD TREE

INGREDIENTS

- just under 2 1/2 cups (220 g) cake flour
- 3/4 cup (160 g) brown sugar
- 7 1/2 tbsp (160 g) honey
- 5.3 oz (150 g) butter
- 1 egg
- 1 tsp ground ginger
- 1 tsp ground cinnamon
- 1/2 tsp ground cloves
- 1/2 tsp ground nutmeg
- 1/2 tsp baking soda
- salt

for the royal icing
- 1/4 cup (160 g) powdered sugar
- 2 tbsp (30 g) egg whites
- 1 tsp lemon juice

for decorating
- silver sugar decorations

Dice the butter and put it in a kitchen mixer with the flour, sugar, and honey. Add the egg, spices, baking soda, and a pinch of salt, and mix thoroughly for 1 minute. Put the dough on a lightly floured work surface and knead until smooth and compact. Make it into a loaf shape, wrap in plastic wrap, and leave to rest in the refrigerator for one hour.

Roll out the dough on a lightly floured work surface, to a thickness of 0.2 in (0.5 cm). With different-shaped star cookie cutters, cut out two shapes for each size. Put the stars on a baking pan lined with parchment paper, and bake at 350°F (180°C) for about 10–12 minutes. Take out of the oven and leave to cool on a cake rack.

For the royal icing: Whisk the egg whites with an electric hand mixer until they are frothy; add the powdered sugar, then the lemon juice, and continue whisking for about 5 minutes. Put the frosting in a pastry bag with a very thin flat-topped nozzle and cover the tops of the cookies, starting with the biggest star. Build the tree by putting the cookies one on top of another, in descending order, covering each layer with icing as you go; garnish each tip with a silver ball. Finish with the smallest star on top, and decorate it with lots of silver sugar decorations (hold the star firmly for at least 5 minutes, so it doesn't fall off). Leave to set completely before serving.

makes 2 trees

> BINGO CARDS

Christmas

INGREDIENTS

for the sweet shortcrust cookies
- 4 egg yolks
- 6 1/4 cups (560 g) cake flour
- 1 1/2 cups (200 g) powdered sugar
- 14 oz (400 g) butter
- 1 tsp vanilla extract

for the royal frosting
- 7 1/4 tbsp (100 g) egg whites
- 4 3/4 cups (600 g) powdered sugar
- red food coloring

for decorating
- 10.6 oz (300 g) white fondant icing
- 3.5 oz (100 g) green fondant icing
- 3.5 oz (100 g) red fondant icing

Prepare the sweet shortcrust pastry following the recipe in the first section of this book. Wrap the dough in plastic wrap and leave in the refrigerator for one hour.

Stretch the pastry to a thickness of about 0.5 in (1 cm), and cut out the shapes of the bingo cards. Put them on a baking pan lined with parchment paper and bake at 325°F (170°C) for about 20 minutes. Leave to cool.

For the frosting: Whisk the egg whites with the powdered sugar until stiff. Put a small amount of frosting in another bowl and add the red food coloring.

Sprinkle the work surface with powdered sugar, roll out the white fondant icing to a thickness of about 0.2 in (0.5 cm), then cut out rectangles the same size as the cookies. Put a little white frosting on top of each cookie and then stick a rectangle of white fondant icing on top. Use the red royal frosting to pipe the boxes and the numbers inside.

Make holly leaves with the green fondant icing and use them to decorate the corners of the cards. Finish with little balls of red royal frosting for the berries. To make the numbers, create little rolls of red fondant icing cut to a thickness of 0.2 in (0.5 cm), then pipe the numbers on top with the white royal icing.

makes 10 cookies

PREPARATION TIME: 90 min   **COOKING TIME:** 20 min

› SPICED WHITE CHOCOLATE CHRISTMAS CAKE

Christmas

Put the ingredients for the batter in a bowl and mix vigorously with a wooden spoon for 5 minutes, or until the ingredients are thoroughly mixed. Grease a round 6 in (15 cm) cake pan with high sides and line it with extra thick parchment paper. Pour in the batter and level the top with the back of a wet tablespoon.

Bake on the middle shelf at 275°F (140°C) for about 90 minutes (if the top of the cake browns too quickly, cover it with foil). Check if it is cooked by pressing lightly on the center of the cake, which must be firm; if it's not ready, bake for another 15 minutes. Take out of the oven and leave to cool completely, then turn it out onto a cake rack.

For the ganache: Finely chop the white chocolate and put it in a bowl. Bring the cream to a boil, pour it over the chocolate, and stir with a whisk until it has completely melted. Leave to cool. When it reaches room temperature, pour it over the entire cake. Decorate how you like with the cinnamon stick, candied cherries, and slices of candied orange peel. Leave to rest for a few hours before serving.

INGREDIENTS
- 1/3 cup (50 g) raisins
- 1 2/3 cups (150 g) cake flour
- 2/3 cup (130 g) brown sugar
- 4 oz (115 g) soft butter
- 5 tbsp (40 g) candied cherries cut in half
- 5 tbsp (40 g) diced candied orange peel
- 7 1/2 tbsp (40 g) ground almonds
- 3 eggs
- 2 tbsp brandy
- 1 tbsp honey
- 1 tsp grated lemon zest
- 1 tsp ground mixed spice (cinnamon, cloves, and ginger)
- 1/2 tsp ground nutmeg

for the white chocolate ganache
- 8.8 oz (250 g) white chocolate
- 1 cup (125 g) fresh cream

for decorating
- candied cherries
- slices of candied orange peel
- 1 cinnamon stick

serves 6

PREPARATION TIME: 30 min   **RESTING TIME:** 2-3 hours   **COOKING TIME:** 90 min

> PANFORTE

INGREDIENTS
- 1 3/4 cups (300 g) unshelled almonds
- 3/4 cup (100 g) candied citron peel
- 3/4 cup (100 g) candied orange peel
- 3/4 cup (100 g) candied melon
- 1 cup (150 g) powdered sugar
- 1 1/2 cups (140 g) all-purpose flour
- 6 2/3 tbsp (100 ml) water
- 7 tbsp (150 g) honey
- 2 tsp (5 g) ground cinnamon
- 1 tsp (2 g) ground cilantro
- 1 tsp (2 g) grated nutmeg
- 1 tsp (2 g) white pepper
- 1/2 tsp (1 g) whole cloves
- 1 vanilla pod

you will also need
- 2 sheets of rice paper
- powdered sugar

Butter and flour a round 9 in (22 cm) springform cake pan. Cut the sheets of rice paper and line the bottom and sides of the cake pan. Toast the almonds in the oven at 250°F (120°C) for about 10 minutes. Put the water, honey, and powdered sugar in a saucepan. Cook over low heat, stirring regularly, until it reaches a temperature of 250°F (120°C).

Chop up a third of the almonds and put them in a bowl with the flour, spices, whole almonds, vanilla seeds, and all the diced candied fruit. Add in the honey syrup and stir vigorously until all the ingredients are mixed together.

Pour the mixture into the cake pan, press it down firmly, and level with the back of a wet tablespoon. Sprinkle generously with powdered sugar and bake at 325°F (170°C) for about 30 minutes. Take out of the oven and leave to cool in the cake pan. Turn it out onto a serving plate, sprinkle with more powdered sugar, and serve.

serves 8-10

PREPARATION TIME: 1 hour   **COOKING TIME:** 30 min

❯ MY RECIPES

> INDEX OF RECIPES

> INDEX OF INGREDIENTS

TEXT
and PHOTOGRAPHS
Alice Cucina

PROJECT EDITORS
Nicole Di Giammatteo
Marta Koral

GRAPHIC DESIGN
Paola Piacco

WHITE STAR PUBLISHERS

White Star Publishers® is a trademark owned by White Star s.r.l.

© 2020 White Star s.r.l.
Piazzale Luigi Cadorna, 6 - 20123 Milan, Italy
www.whitestar.it

ISBN 978-88-544-1690-1
1 2 3 4 5 6   24 23 22 21 20

Translation: TperTradurre s.r.l.

Printed in Italy by Rotolito S.p.A. - Seggiano di Pioltello (MI)